O Taste and See:

Food Poems

Edited by

David Lee Garrison

& Terry Hermsen

As the Englishman wakes [Hanna] bends over his body
and places a third of the plum into his mouth. His mouth holds it,
like water, the jaw not moving.

He looks as if he will cry from this pleasure. She can
sense the plum being swallowed.

He brings his hand up and wipes from his lip the last
dribble, which his tongue cannot reach, and puts his finger in his
mouth to suck it. Let me tell you about plums, he says....

-Michael Ondaatje, *The English Patient*

Harmony Series
Bottom Dog Press
Huron, Ohio

Bottom Dog Press, Inc.
PO Box 425
Huron, Ohio 44839
http://members.aol.com/lsmithdog/bottomdog
Director& General Editor: Larry Smith
Lsmithdog@aol.com

Cover Design & Drawings by
Erin Johnson of Chicago

Credits and Acknowledgments are listed on page 191.
We thank the editors, publishers, and poets for the rights to reproduce
their work here.
All poems are covered by copyright and may not be reproduced without
written permission from original publishers.

We thank the Ohio Arts Council for its continued support.

Ohio Arts Council
A STATE AGENCY
THAT SUPPORTS PUBLIC
PROGRAMS IN THE ARTS

INTRODUCTION

When Charles Wilson Peale, one of America's first successful artists, painted his "Exhumation of the Mastodon" in 1801, he imagined himself representing the great conquering of the world by science and art. His eldest son Raphaelle, on the other hand, painted mostly still-lifes of common household realities, including food—blackberries and watermelons, peaches, and slabs of meat. Peale was disappointed with his son's choice of subject matter because he held to a common view that historical subjects and portraits of famous people and events expressed the grandeur of humanity, and that still-lifes were mere sketches of the everyday—domestic and mundane.

Two centuries later, has that changed? Are we ready to look at still-lifes—or read poems about food—in a way that people in the early days of our country were not? Have we turned the equation around and come to see in everyday things the depth of our existence? This book, in a quiet way, suggests just that. It asks us to examine with words, as carefully as Raphaelle Peale did with his brush, the sources of sustenance, of memory and community that food brings to our lives, whether in the form of hamburgers or kibbe, mushrooms dug from the forest floor or wine aged in vats and cellars.

It began, tellingly enough, in a cafeteria line at the Antioch Writers' Workshop, when we turned to each other and said, "Hey, we could do an anthology of poems about food!" Little did we know the wealth of poems that would pour into our mailboxes as we began work on our first book, *Food Poems*, and again when we called for submissions for this one, which grew from it.

Perhaps the number of poems written now about food has to do with a number of deep collective wishes: to return to our roots, as well as to savor slower, more diverse tastes…to reflect on how far we've come from the simpler plantings and gardenings that consumed our days less than a century ago…to scrape past the shiny packaging that encloses food in our supermarkets…to lift up one single orb before us—a beet, an onion, a peach, a cluster of blackberries…to taste again, as one poet puts it, "the work of summer's earth."

What does food tell us in these poems?

It tells us our heritage—recipes for soup and pie, odes to beets and mackerel and stew, different words for rice in Chinese, customs associated with the roasting of green chile peppers in the American Southwest, a mother's Sunday morning habit of standing "in a slip / lost in blues, / and those collards, / wild-eared, / singing."

It tells us who we were. One poet remembers being taken on lunch dates with her working mother in an era when most women stayed home. Another reaches back to our Paleolithic past, when we were lean because we foraged; we still like to forage, as we realize in "Learning to Clam." Nor are we far away in time from the anthropophagic horrors of the Donner Party of pioneers. And although we have been gardeners for centuries, we now see the garden not as "survival / and beans in February—but a transitory haven / for vegetables, flowers, birds, your eyes."

It tells us about love. Several of these poems begin in the kitchen and end in the bedroom where we learn "The Art of Love."

It tells us about our rituals. Communion is spiritual food, even in an asylum. The all-night diner is a uniquely American shrine where we find out "how good greasy tastes." The dinner party's customs and traditions bring us another kind of communal joy, just as eating pie and drinking coffee with her mother and her mother's friends represent a ritual of transition from girlhood to womanhood for a child of thirteen.

It tells us about giving and gorging. A man raised in hunger and want feeds stray cats. A daughter recognizes the gift she received by witnessing her mother's generosity to hobos. A visitor describes a Midwestern meal "washed down with peach cobblers, / coconut pie, sighing under vanilla / ice cream in a scoop...."

It tells us of the sweetness and abundance of life—fresh-picked peaches, ripe tomatoes "like joyful, bursting hearts," the ice cream you buy from a truck that melts as you eat it"—and the saltiness in the air at the fish market.

It tells us what might have been: "I often wonder, / had I been born beautiful, / a Venus on the California seashore, / if I'd have learned to eat and drink so well?"

It tells us that reading can make us hungry, that a beard can be "stained purple / by the word *juice*," that a poem is "like a piece of bread and butter" or like soup prepared from "rutabaga, sore toe, a sudden / drop in barometric pressure, / rich Minnesota farmland...."

It tells us that we need poetry as much as we need food.

Let the feast begin.

- David Lee Garrison and Terry Hermsen

CONTENTS

III. FAMILY 49

IV. GARDEN 67

V. STORIES **85**

VI. ODES **103**

VII. LOVE **117**

VIII. MARKET   141

IX. WORLD   **161**

This book is for all of our families.

friends

O Taste and See   by Denise Levertov

The world is
not with us enough.
O taste and see

the subway Bible poster said,
meaning **The Lord**, meaning
if anything all that lives
to the imagination's tongue,

grief, mercy, language,
tangerine, weather, to
breathe them, bite,
savor, chew, swallow, transform

into our flesh our
deaths, crossing the street, plum, quince,
living in the orchard and being

hungry, and plucking
the fruit.

Ode to the Tomato   by Pablo Neruda
translated by David Lee Garrison

The street
filled up with tomatoes,
noon,
summer,
the light
splits
in two tomato
halves
and the juice
runs
down the streets.

In December
the tomato
breaks loose,
invading
kitchens,
stealing into lunches,
lounging
on sideboards and
in between glasses,
butter dishes,
blue salt shakers.
It has
its own light,
benign majesty.
We must, unfortunately,
murder it:
the knife
sinks
into its living flesh,
it's a red
viscera,
a cool
sun,
deep,
limitless,
it fills the salads
of Chile,
marrying happily
the bright onion,
and to celebrate,
we let oil,
child
and essence of the olive,
pour down
over its open hemispheres,
pepper
adds
its fragrance,
salt its magnetism:
these are the weddings
of the day,

parsley
raises
its flags,
potatoes
boil vigorously,
roasting meat
bangs
on the door
with its aroma,
it's time!
let's eat!
and on
the table, on the waist
of summer
the tomato,
astro of the earth,
fertile,
ever multiplying
star,
reveals to us
its orbits,
its canals,
its distinguished plenitude
and boneless,
heartless,
armorless
abundance,
brings to us
the gift
of its fiery color
and the integrity
of its freshness.

Sestina

by Elizabeth Bishop

September rain falls on the house.
In the failing light, the old grandmother
sits in the kitchen with the child
beside the Little Marvel Stove,
reading the jokes from the almanac,
laughing and talking to hide her tears.

She thinks that her equinoctial tears
and the rain that beats on the roof of the house
were both foretold by the almanac,
but only known to a grandmother.
The iron kettle sings on the stove.
She cuts some bread and says to the child,

It's time for tea now; but the child
is watching the teakettle's small hard tears
dance like mad on the hot black stove,
the way the rain must dance on the house.
Tidying up, the old grandmother
hangs up the clever almanac

on its string. Birdlike, the almanac
hovers half open above the child,
hovers above the old grandmother
and her teacup full of dark brown tears.
She shivers and says she thinks the house
feels chilly, and puts more wood in the stove.

It was to be, says the Marvel Stove.
I know what I know, says the almanac.
With crayons the child draws a rigid house
and a winding pathway. Then the child
puts in a man with buttons like tears
and shows it proudly to the grandmother.

But secretly, while the grandmother
busies herself about the stove,

the little moons fall down like tears
from between the pages of the almanac
in the the flower bed the child
has carefully placed in the front of the house.

Time to plant tears, says the almanac.
The grandmother sings to the marvelous stove
and the child draws another inscrutable house.

After Apple-Picking   by Robert Frost

My long two-pointed ladder's sticking through a tree
Toward heaven still,
And there's a barrel that I didn't fill
Beside it, and there may be two or three
Apples I didn't pick upon some bough.
But I am done with apple-picking now.
Essence of winter sleep is on the night,
The scent of apples: I am drowsing off.
I cannot rub the strangeness from my sight
I got from looking through a pane of glass
I skimmed this morning from the drinking trough
And held against the world of hoary grass.
It melted, and I let it fall and break.
But I was well
Upon my way to sleep before it fell,
And I could tell
What form my dreaming was about to take.
Magnified apples appear and disappear,
Stem end and blossom end,
and every fleck of russet showing clear.
My instep arch not only keeps the ache,
It keeps the pressure of a ladder-round.
I feel the ladder sway as the boughs bend.
And I keep hearing from the cellar bin
The rumbling sound
Of load on load of apples coming in.
For I have had too much

of apple-picking: I am overtired
Of the great harvest I myself desired.
There were ten thousand thousand fruits to touch,
Cherish in hand, lift down, and not let fall.
For all
That struck the earth,
No matter if not bruised or spiked with stubble,
Went surely to the cider-apple heap
As of no worth.
One can see what will trouble
This sleep of mine, whatever sleep it is.
Were he not gone,
The woodchuck could say whether it's like his
Long sleep, as I describe its coming on,
Or just some human sleep.

Selections from *Tender Buttons*   by Gertrude Stein

RHUBARB.

Rhubarb is susan not susan not seat in bunch toys not wild and laugh-
able not in little places not in neglect and vegetable not in fold coal age
not please.

SINGLE FISH.

Single fish single fish single fish egg-plant single fish sight.
A sweet win and not less noisy than saddle and more ploughing and
nearly well painted by little things so.
Please shade it a play. It is necessary and beside the large sort is puff.
Every way oakly, please prune it near. It is so found.
It is not the same.

CAKE.

Cake cast in went to be and needles wine needles are such.

This is today. A can experiment is that which makes a town, makes a town dirty, it is little please. We came back. Two bore, bore what, a mussed ash, ash when there is tin. This meant cake. It was a sign.

Another time there was extra a hat pin sought long and this dark made a display. The result was yellow. A caution, not a caution to be.

It is no use to cause a foolish number. A blanket stretch a cloud, a shame, all that bakery can tease, all that is beginning and yesterday yesterday we had it met. It means some change. No some day.

A little leaf upon a scene an ocean any where there, a bland and likely in the stream a recollection green land. Why white.

CUSTARD.

Custard is this. It has aches, aches when. Not to be. Not to be narrowly. This makes a whole little hill.

It is better than a little thing that has mellow real mellow. It is better than lakes whole lakes, it is better than seeding.

POTATOES.

Real potatoes cut in between.

POTATOES.

In the preparation of cheese, in the preparation of crackers, in the preparation of butter, in it.

ROAST POTATOES.

Roast potatoes for.

ASPARAGUS.

Asparagus in a lean in a lean to hot. This makes it art and it is wet wet weather wet weather wet.

To Wine   **by Louise Bogan**

Cup, ignorant and cruel,
Take from the mandate, love,
Its urgency to prove
Unfaith, renewal.

Take from the mind its loss:
The lipless dead that lie
Face upward in the earth,
Strong hand and slender thigh;
Return to the vein
All that is worth
Grief. Give that beat again.

A Step Away from Them   **by Frank O'Hara**

It's my lunch hour, so I go
for a walk among the hum-colored
cabs. First, down the sidewalk
where laborers feed their dirty
glistening torsos sandwiches
and Coca-Cola, with yellow helmets
on. They protect them from falling
bricks, I guess. Then onto the
avenue where skirts are flipping
above heels and blow up over
grates. The sun is hot, but the
cabs stir up the air. I look
at bargains in wristwatches. There
are cats playing in sawdust.
                                              On
to Times Square, where the sign
blows smoke over my head, and higher
the waterfall pours lightly. A
Negro stands in a doorway with a

toothpick, languorously agitating.
A blonde chorus girl clicks: he
smiles and rubs his chin. Everything
suddenly honks: it is 12:40 of
a Thursday.
        Neon in daylight is a
great pleasure, as Edwin Denby would
write, as are light bulbs in daylight.
I stop for a cheeseburger at JULIET'S
CORNER. Giulietta Masina, wife of
Federico Felline, *è bell' attrice.*

And chocolate malted. A lady in
foxes on such a day puts her poodle
in a cab.
        There are several Puerto
Ricans on the avenue today, which
makes it beautiful and warm. First
Bunny died, then John Latouche,
then Jackson Pollock. But is the
earth as full as life was full, of them?
And one has eaten and one walks,
past the magazines with nudes
and the posters for BULLFIGHT and
the Manhattan Storage Warehouse,
which they'll soon tear down. I
used to think they had the Armory
Show there.
        A glass of papaya juice
and back to work. My heart is in my
pocket, it is Poems by Pierre Reverdy.

1956

A Supermarket in California   by Allen Ginsberg

What thoughts I have of you tonight, Walt Whitman, for I walked down
the sidestreets under the trees with a headache self-conscious looking at
the full moon.

In my hungry fatigue, and shopping for images, I went into the neon
fruit supermarket, dreaming of your enumerations!

What peaches and what penumbras! Whole families shopping at night!
Aisles full of husbands! Wives in the avocados, babies in the tomatoes—
and you, García Lorca, what were you doing down by the watermelons?

I saw you, Walt Whitman, childless, lonely old grubber, poking among
the meats in the refrigerator and eyeing the grocery boys.

I heard you asking questions of each: Who killed the pork chops?
What price bananas? Are you my Angel?

I wandered in and out of the brilliant stacks of cans following you, and
followed in my imagination by the store detective.

We strode down the open corridors together in our solitary fancy
tasting artichokes, possessing every frozen delicacy, and never passing
the cashier.

Where are we going, Walt Whitman? The doors close in an hour.
Which way does your beard point tonight?

(I touch your book and dream of our odyssey in the supermarket and
feel absurd.)

Will we walk all night through solitary streets? The trees add shade to
shade, lights out in the houses, we'll both be lonely.

Will we stroll dreaming of the lost America of love past blue automo-
biles in driveways, home to our silent cottage?

Ah, dear father, graybeard, lonely old courage-teacher, what America
did you have when Charon quit poling his ferry and you got out on a
smoking bank and stood watching the boat disappear on the black waters
of Lethe?

Berkeley, 1955/1956

Northern Pike   **by James Wright**

All right. Try this,
Then. Every body
I know and care for,
And every body
Else is going
To die in a loneliness
I can't imagine and a pain
I don't know. We had
To go on living. We
Untangled the net, we slit
The body of this fish
Open from the hinge of the tail
To a place beneath the chin
I wish I could sing of.
I would just as soon we let
The living go on living.
An old poet whom we believe in
Said the same thing, and so
We paused among the dark cattails and prayed
For the muskrats,
For the ripples below their tails,
For the little movements that we knew the crawdads were making under
          water,
For the right-hand wrist of my cousin who is a policeman.
We prayed for the game warden's blindness.
We prayed for the road home.
We ate the fish.
There must be something very beautiful in my body,
I am so happy.

This Is Just To Say   by William Carlos Williams

I have eaten
the plums
that were in
the icebox

and which
you were probably
saving
for breakfast

Forgive me
they were delicious
so sweet
and so cold

recipes

Soup

by Maggie Anderson

I make soup and name the seasonings:
parsley, the damp tears that,
homesick, I planted in the loved earth.
Tiny black pepper eyes. Mice in the walls,
the bullets we will have to bite,
sharp clove stars inside the blue pillow
I put over my feet every night
so nothing gets away. I add
sweet basil, mint or saint;
a small procession of bay leaf,
laurel. Salt stream, salt water,
sea anemone. The chatter of barnacles
stuck to the rocks, gull cry and kestrel.
Chicken carcass, soft bone marrow,
once feathered, this bed
for vegetables I know to speak to:
the riven onions, train whistle.
Limp celery stalks I hold up to the light
and try to see through, cold hands.
Potato skins, weathered leather,
cinched saddles and compost.
Rutabaga, sore toe, a sudden
drop in barometric pressure,
rich Minnesota farmland
where yellow leaves were swept
across the burned fields.
What floats through the blue air
is feathers, is white rice,
falling into pottage, into hunger,
wet snow that vanishes,
the steaming ground.

Salt   **by Susan Kelly-DeWitt**

People still die for it.
        Gandhi marched to the sea
        for it. The heart spasms

        without it, the muscles cramp.
Last night I sobbed crazily
and the salt appeared on cue,

residue of fifty years.
        The body floats in it.
        The oceans are drenched in it.

So,
the soul must feel
        at home in it,

        among the measuring
        spoons and shakers,
among the bitter, shining

crystals of salt—
        even in the Great Salt
        Desert. Boil

        any pot of water
and all your plans will vanish
except for the salts.

Kibbe

by Susan Azar Porterfield

Today in the land of new-world corn,
heart of the Midwest, I'm making kibbe.

I'll need pine nuts and minced lamb,
cinnamon bark from an East India tree,

and bulghur, which my father called,
as I do, by its Arabic name.

The sound slips from my tongue,
and already onion and pignolias,

allspice, butter-browned, scent the house.
Already I'm wrapped in the alleys

of Beirut where murmurs drift from kitchens
of women who look like me.

Our genius is in the dish,
and in the dish made word.

Years ago, oil and figs, papyrus
and purple dye sailed from Byblos

to Athens to Rome. Now *olive,*
bread, wine can send us reeling.

Someone is always making kibbe.
Tomorrow a daughter in Damascus

will make it. The day after,
a mother in Jenin.

Gift of Flour by Susan Jelus

Today men are delivering flour to the widows of Yellow Springs: one ton
in 10-pound bags of powder—a slave's bequest carried forward 100 years.
Most widows hate the gift the first year:
> the sacks too full, too still,

creased and sagging in daylight.
Later, they add brown sugar, raisins, crack an egg: plop, roll, cut,
lick batter from one finger, embellish. Time passes: through the channel
there is a black face at the door—into the kitchen canyon:
> bathrobe, limbs, warm oven, the blending and working of dust.

Mustard Greens by Karen Rigby

I.

coiled *choy*
in the glazed pan,
loud language
stir-frying

II.

in the kitchens
of every continent
women open
the necks
of their blouses

III.

yellow buds fuel
the god
of wholesale
longing

IV.

under the knife's
instruction,
stalks loosen
their hold

V.

mustard
greens taste
like potato
and tubular rose

VI.

broad leaves turn
in the green-lit
backwash
of a tortoise

Borscht

by Karen Rigby

Throw a bone in the crock.
Cut onions, bon-voyage streamers,
rub tendons with marjoram
and cabbage soft enough to tear

on my tongue. Give me
the good stink of root cellar
and white night, soup so crimson
I could paint the walls:

blood from the mink farms,
hands riveting bolts
to the gunwale of a ship.
Public beatings in Yevtushenko's
Babi Yar. Borscht steams

like a horse combed to a rich gloss
for the May Day parade.
Once, on a tour of the Orthodox domes,
a bicyclist rode past balancing

his green gardener's pail
between the handlebars.
Potatoes and a newborn dog
bedded on newsprint.
The man could hardly steer

with the weight of his gifts.
Country of exiles, bath houses,
blood of the czars—
I raise the bowl and drink
to the steppe's red beets.

Green Chile   by Jimmy Santiago Baca

I prefer red chile over my eggs
and potatoes for breakfast.
Red chile *ristras* decorate my door,
dry on my roof, and hang from eaves.
They lend open-air vegetable stands
historical grandeur, and gently swing
with an air of festive welcome.
I can hear them talking in the wind,
haggard, yellowing, crisp, rasping
tongues of old men, licking the breeze.

            But grandmother loves green chile.
When I visit her,
she holds the green chile pepper
in her wrinkled hands.
Ah, voluptuous, masculine,
an air of authority and youth simmers
from its swan-neck stem, tapering to a flowery
collar, fermenting resinous spice.
A well-dressed gentleman at the door
my grandmother takes sensuously in her hand,
rubbing its firm glossed sides,
caressing the oily rubbery serpent,
with mouth-watering fulfillment,
fondling its curves with gentle fingers.
Its bearing magnificent and taut
as flanks of a tiger in mid-leap,
she thrusts her blade into
and cuts it open, with lust
on her hot mouth, sweating over the stove,
bandanna round her forehead,
Mysterious passion on her face
as she serves me green chile con carne
between soft warm leaves of corn tortillas,
with beans and rice—her sacrifice
to her little prince.
I slurp from my plate
with a last bit of tortilla, my mouth burns
and I hiss and drink a tall glass of cold water.

All over New Mexico, sunburned men and women
drive rickety trucks stuffed with gunny-sacks
of green chile, from Belen, Veguita, Willard, Estancia,
San Antonio y Socorro, from fields
to roadside stands, you see them roasting green chile
in screen-sided homemade barrels, and for a dollar a bag,
we relive this old, beautiful ritual again and again.

Fondue   **by Robert Flanagan**
                        for Scott Sommer

I try to skewer two chunks of raw meat, and the fork
leaps into a third—my hand
quivers in pain on the barbed hooks,
fingers opening and closing like the mouth
of a dying carp.

Meat in the pot of oil
sends off a smell of burning hair, a mammoth
screams away the click of cufflinks and earrings,
and my struck hand casts its shadow on the wall,
a cave painting.

Bread & Sauce   **by Thom Tammaro**
 Serves One

Ingredients:
1 slice favorite bread
1 large spoonful (preferably wooden) favorite sauce

Sunday. 6:00 a.m. I cannot give you the waking up to the aroma of my
mother's sauce simmering in a metal pot in the kitchen on the other side
of the house. I cannot give you the aroma of peeled, ripe tomatoes
bathing in olive oil, garlic, the spicy marriage of oregano, basil, parsley,
salt, pepper, sugar, and an onion buoying in a bubbling ocean of red. I
cannot give you the sound of sauce bubbles rising to the oily surface and

popping. And I cannot give you the muffled sound of a half-cup of water being poured into this too-fast thickening sauce. Nor can I give you my mother, standing at the stove, stirring the saucy whirlpool or the dull thud and click of a long-handled wooden spoon against the metal sides of the sauce pot.

And least of all, I cannot give you a young boy's delight as he bites into a slice of white bread spread thick and hot and dark red with that sauce— the mother's way of staving off raging appetites when, on Sunday mornings after Mass, the children arrived home famished, the wafery host feeding other appetites, their stomachs hollow and growling from the night-before-Eucharistic-fast, and the never-arriving 1:00 p. m. macaroni dinner lay like an oasis on the other side of a great, uncrossable desert,

"Careful! You'll burn your tongue!" she cautioned us, or:

"Basta!" or:

"Tenzione! You'll burn the roof of your mouth!"

And we did.

We cannot live by bread alone. But by bread and sauce we could live forever!

So here is what I can give you—this directive: spread one wooden ladle of your favorite tomato sauce[*] on a slice of your favorite bread.[**]

Sunday, 1:00 p.m. A voice is calling you to the dinner table. You have survived another Sunday morning famine. Give us this day our daily bread (and sauce). Grazie a Dio! *Mangiare!*

[*] (It would be foolish of me to offer you my Mother's recipe for tomato sauce, for undoubtedly it would fall short of your favorite sauce because all of your life your mother or your father's sauce has been the litmus test against which all sauces have been measured and, invariably, have failed!)

[**] (Even that perfectly-shaped slice of plain, tasteless, glutinous, inexpensive, white wonder sandwich bread that you ate in your school lunches throughout your childhood will be miraculously transubstantiated!)

Macaroni & Cheese Survey   **by Terry Kirts**

In the mail this morning, a certified letter:

Your household has been selected to participate

in a very important study about macaroni and cheese.

And I think about the blue and white box, the pouch
of day-glo powder, the lonely square of margarine melting
into golden rivulets in the murky white saucepan. I remember
those Lenten nights, after stations of the cross, eating quietly
and pondering the scourging, all of Jesus' falling,
the long blue cloth Veronica held up to wipe his face.
When do you usually eat macaroni and cheese?
After I have sinned. No, really, on cold winter nights
when a scalding bath is not enough to keep me warm,
when I wear sweatshirts and two pairs of socks, I cradle
the hot pan in my lap and I devour every crusty morsel
intended for eight or ten or twelve, the little numbers
of the nutrition chart rising like stock prices in my head.
Whom do you usually eat macaroni and cheese with?
With Troy, the day I fainted and the doctor suggested
something soft. With Grandma, in Rest Haven
Nursing Home, two weeks before she died. But almost
no one lately, despite its forced mythology in grade school
and its seasonal names—the puns about elbows and tubes.
I loved it then, but it could not cover up the overcooked peas
I would not eat while the lunch room monitor stood guard.
The other kids ran off laughing to kick ball as I gagged,
scraped the tray into a bucket, and hung my head.
Please write in how many people are usually present
when you eat macaroni and cheese. Surely there
were a thousand in the auto-smorgasbord in Terre Haute,
where a vast sea of casseroles strolled by on conveyors.
Could the loaves and fishes have fed as many, we wondered,
dazzled into belief under buzzing fluorescents? Lean, angelic
women in hair nets and white polyester attended our needs:
snowy peaks of whipped potatoes, gurgling bogs of gravy,
and the celestial sheen of the macaroni pan, gleaming through

the crowd like a familiar planet, a storybook image of Oz.
*When buying macaroni and cheese, do you buy it because
it is an. . .* opiate of the complacent masses? retrograde symbol
of a simpler youth? foil to haute cuisine? savior of housewives
and bachelors? The woman at work says she swears by
Patti LaBelle's recipe, after she made it on Oprah, the way
the Velveeta does not curdle in the oven or burn, the way Patti
honored her strong mother that day with a song, how the diva—
the divine prima donna in sequins and yards of purple tulle—put her
microphone aside, donned an apron, and got her hands and fingers
dirty making macaroni and cheese *right before our very eyes.*

Where There's Smoke, There's Dinner   by Edmund Conti

Modern day cooking
Is easy and fun.
When the smoke alarm
Goes off, it's done.

Blueberries   by Edmund Conti

There's never enough in
A blueberry muffin.

Summer Haiku   by Edmund Conti

Sweet corn for dinner
Grinning
From ear to ear

Preserves

by Gabriel Welsch

I cut back my shriveled garden this November,
all fruits gone, leaves frost crunched but fragrant
with the last stores of water rising to the snipped stems.
In other yards, scarfed gardeners bundle stakes,
cast neat squares with winter rye,
are soundless but for movement, harvest
long plucked like the mills and jobs
that built these homes. They snug potatoes
for winter, firm the mounds over onions,
while I cut back the odd ornament of roses,
lady's mantle, thyme and lavender.

Through these softened Appalachians,
western Pennsylvania towns crouch half hollow,
Main Street a straight shot to foundries and old rails
bleeding rust into the gravel, scrub dead
grass and bent underbrush by the turnpike.
People here wrinkle against the cold. They still
can, put up food, cure meat, hunt and hold church
bake sales, dances, festivals, card games. They
keep shelves of pillowy pears, firmed apple butter,
cabbage pressed to glass and tomatoes
glistening with stymied sun.

On these coldest days, snow is like dust,
twisting glass ghosting along salt routed
pavement and stretches of potholes.
The windows of downtown darken with emptiness
so deep I see the back walls of former stores.
Farm fences mimic hillocks at sight's edge,
where the sky is opaque milk crusted dry, and I see
only the slow steps of people in the fog,
grey as ghostly poplar trunks, hunched
shadows heavier than the cold's
pale or the wind-worn stone of storefronts.

On those days, I understand their pantry shelves,
and why my wife wicks summer into a Ball jar.
We want to smell the work of summer's

earth, our home when green and warm.
I crouched one day last August and pruned
the shrubby lavender stems pouched in blue,
stripped the stems and packed the buds
in a jar with alcohol gurgling deep. We left
the jar for months in our tight pantry,
among artichoke hearts and olives,
keeping it like food.

This winter, amid the buffeting brown and gray,
dulled by the dour churches and salt scud,
wrinkled truck drivers and breath smoked
with cold, I opened the jar, and the smell
plopped out, spicy-thick and vibrant
as the day I picked it, drenched in alcohol
that normally kills, preserving an essence
like light captured in silver, a photograph
of a smell. The foreign musk mingled with steel,
the rot of frost kill, canning steam and the whiff
of stored cabbage, all sharpened by cold.

My Mother's Pie Crust   by Barbara Crooker

Light as angels' breath, shatters into flakes
with each forkful, never soggy-bottomed
or scorched on top, the lattices evenly woven,
pinched crimps an inch apart.
My ex-husband said he'd eat grasshoppers
if my mother baked them in a pie.
Smooth tart lemon, froth of meringue.
Apples dusted with cinnamon, nutmeg.
Pumpkin that cracks in the middle
of its own weight. Mine are good,
but not like hers, though I keep trying,
rolling the dough this way and that, dusting
the cloth with flour. "You have to chill the Crisco,"
she says. "You need a light touch
to keep it tender; too much handling
makes a tough crust."

Gather the scraps, make a ball in your hands,
press into a circle. Spread thickly with butter,
sprinkle with cinnamon sugar, roll up, slice, bake.
The strange marriage of fat, flour, and salt
is annealed to ethereal bites. Heaven is attainable,
and the chimes of the timer bring us to the table.

Recipe for Apple Pie   **by David Lee Garrison**

hold the paring knife
to your lips   take a peel
with your tongue   squeeze
the redness into your mouth
slice the sunshine   add
the glisten of sugar   bake
until the smell knocks
on the oven door   cinnamon
nutmeg   dough   the flavor of fall
open the oven   open your home
to the wind of an orchard
to that cozy fire
inside you   then eat
the circle   hot and sweet

Tiramisù   **by Ingrid Wendt**
            for Emmanuel Hatzantonis

"*Tiramisù*: Pick me up," you translated for us,
but "Heaven on earth" is what I for some reason remembered,
and so it was:

            layers of chocolate sponge cake drenched with rum
and espresso; layers of *Mascapone*—cream cheese, *à la Italia*—
thickly topped with shavings of bittersweet chocolate:
                              one more
treat we hadn't dreamed possible, that night you led us through

cobbled back streets of Perugia, fearless in shadows deep below
Medieval walls built, you told us, on Roman walls built on what
Etruscans left behind:

                          such mysteries, glorious beyond
our simple tourist imaginations that night you guided us to your
own favorite restaurant, ordered squash blossom fritters and stuffed
fried olives,

        other surprises picking us up the way that very morning
you'd lifted our spirits of all the weight of the glories of Florence
with melon, *proscuitto*, four kinds of bread you'd shopped for
before we were even awake:

                          friends of just a few days
feeling we'd known you for years—the way all students and colleagues
in your presence lived vivid and true and full of moment:

all of us trusting that all Dante's circles of Hell mattered
no more than one whose heart you would keep from breaking: the one
wanting to go home early; another whose boyfriend let her down:

none of us dreaming beyond the gift of your life,
that it should be taken
back, without notice.
Beyond comprehension, these divers
picking you up, out of the river.

Your own layers of grief beneath all of that love,
impossible. None of us dreaming it there.

Acceptance Speech   **by Lynn Powell**

The radio's replaying last night's winners
and the gratitude of the glamorous,
everyone thanking everybody for making everything
so possible, until I want to shush
the faucet, dry my hands, join in right here
at the cluttered podium of the sink, and thank

my mother for teaching me the true meaning of okra,
my children for putting back the growl in hunger,
my husband, *primo uomo* of dinner, for not
begrudging me this starring role—

without all of them, I know this soup
would not be here tonight.

And let me just add that I could not
have made it without the marrow bone, that blood-
brother to the broth, and the tomatoes
who opened up their hearts, and the self-effacing limas,
the blonde sorority of corn, the cayenne
and oregano who dashed in
in the nick of time.

Special thanks, as always, to the salt—
you know who you are — and to the knife,
who revealed the ripe beneath the rind,
the clean truth underneath the dirty peel.

—I hope I've not forgotten anyone—
oh, yes, to the celery and the parsnip,
those bit players only there to swell the scene,
let me just say: sometimes I know exactly how you feel.

But not tonight, not when it's all
coming to something and the heat is on and
I'm basking in another round
of blue applause.

Kitchen Logistics   by Lois Beebe Hayna

Each morning she reached for her spoon,
heavy and huge, its handle warped
from the steamy heat of thousands
of stews and soups, porridges
and puddings.

As the big spoon stirred and mixed
and beat, it foretold
what lay ahead. If it slipped
from her hand to the table, she knew
someone hungry was on the way.
She'd put on a pot of stew
and stir up biscuits, ready to feed
a ravenous stranger.

If the spoon fell to the floor bowl-up,
she watched for a pleasant surprise. If it landed
bowl-down, she braced for bad news.
She cautioned me never, never
never pick up a spoon left-handed,
and I don't to this day,
though I can't remember what spoon-doom
she said I'd invoke if I did.

When they auctioned her meager goods
her spoon
fell from a cluttered box
bowl-down.

Words, Like Rice and Snow   by Daryl Ngee Chinn

"My rice always comes out too mushy," said Laurie.
Use less water, I told her. "But the recipe says
two cups of water for each cup of rice." Forget
the recipe, I said. Just enough water

to cover your knuckles.

In a Chinese restaurant, once, my brother ordered
for my sister, me, and him. "Three bowls
of uncooked rice," he said in Chinese
to the waiter, who hesitated
and brought us steaming cooked rice.

In college anthropology, Dr. Dietz
mentioned to us eight hundred students that Eskimos
use twenty-two names for snow. He didn't tell us
what any of those words were.

Across the bay from San Francisco, in El Cerrito,
there wasn't much snow where Granma was living
with Mom and Dad. Nor was there much
in the Pearl River delta near Canton, China, where Dad
and Granma grew up. So I asked them about the Chinese
words for rice.

Granma said she was too tired to remember.
Soon she was going to sleep anyway,
so why bother? I waited
until she started to eat lunch with Dad,
and then I asked again. At first,
they were quiet. It was forty years
since either had been back. Then

Dad spread his hands to show how tall
shoots and plants and stalks grew
before they changed names or had to be thinned
or cut. Only poor people ate brown rice, he said.

Granma forgot her lunch, got up, hit her head
on the hanging lamp, moved back and forth,
bent again and again over the floor,
pulled up and put down
shoots on Mom's patterned linoleum.
She said you had to stoop all day
in a field flooded ankle deep

and take each shoot from down in the mud
and put it somewhere else in the mud, *aiee ya*,
growing rice was such hard and tiring work.
Uncooked rice, cooked rice, rice crust, rice porridge,
rice crust broth, rice flour, rice noodles—

I asked my father how to say hello
in Chinese. All he knew
was the English word with his shy lilt
and, " Have you eaten any rice?"
Yesterday we had guests at dinner,
snow fungus soup, steamed chicken,
bean threads and Chinese sausage,
broccoli and black mushrooms in oyster sauce,
rice. My wife had gone to pick up our daughter
from rehearsal, and everyone was eating fast
so we could go to a movie. When Annette,
the babysitter, came early, I opened the door.
"Have you eaten yet?" I asked.

family

The Morning Baking   by Carolyn Forché

Grandma, come back, I forgot
How much lard for these rolls

Think you can put yourself in the ground
Like plain potatoes and grow in Ohio?
I am damn sick of getting fat like you

Think you can lie through your Slovak?
Tell filthy stories about the blood sausage?
Pish-pish nights at the virgin in Detroit?

I blame your raising me up for my Slav tongue
You beat me up out back, taught me to dance

I'll tell you I don't remember any kind of bread
Your wavy loaves of flesh
Stink through my sleep
The stars on your silk robes

But I'm glad I'll look when I'm old
Like a gypsy dusha hauling milk

A Litany of Toast   by Cathy Lentes

Come sit at my Grandmother's table…
let your elbows rest, cool and damp,
on the scrubbed red oilcloth.

Before you a bowl of butter,
fat yellow sticks
cut and jumbled like stones,
honey clinging to comb,
jam and jelly
sealed in paraffin tombs.

A clatter of spoons,
the dance of grease on an iron pan,
the tender crack and sizzle as
morning splits open again.
Her hands blessing the stove,
she murmurs, mindful of toast.

Now, on a plate, heavy and broad,
steaming eggs like sunshine,
thick planks of bacon,
bread, crisp and golden,
butter spread crust to crust.
Eat, she says, *eat.*

Feed on her gospel before you.

Thanksgiving Table   by Ayelet Amittay

At the head, my grandfather,
the sharp protrusions of his elbows
taking too much room; my brother
kicking the table leg, as if
a faster beat could speed up time;
my mother, wan-faced from her vigil
over pots; grandma muttering
rude asides under her breath;
and the space beside me
where my father
                used to sit,
close to the kitchen door, so that he
could lean far back in his chair
to fit us in his camera's frame.
All of us, the plates, cups, cornbread,
turkey steeped in all its trimmings,
even the dog, held upright, squirming
had its place. All that he loved,
compressed. He held that camera
like a sleeping child;

it gained weight in his palm, became
a measure of what one man's life
can hold,
        and then let fall. The years
slide under us, but this day hangs
frozen: the table stacked with food,
our smiles opening
toward him like hands.

Lunch Dates   **by Gail Bellamy**

We had a rendezvous
each noon,
my mother and I,
at the soda fountain
of Nate's Pharmacy
where she bought me
burgers and phosphates
soup and hot dogs
grilled cheese and fries,
where she watched me
eat apples for dessert
then kissed me goodbye
at the bus stop
before I walked
back to school and
she rode back to
her job at the paper.
Well fed, well loved, much envied
I thought myself
until at age 10
I had lunch at my friend
Laurel's house
where in front of the TV
we ate baloney sandwiches
and chocolate chip cookies
made with margarine
while her mother drank

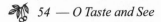

instant Nescafe in the kitchen
with a neighbor woman.
I heard them talking about me:
"Poor little thing...her mother works."

Adolescence   **by Kevin Prufer**

The little sleep in the melon, the seeds
swaying on strings in the hollow of it,
rolled from a brown bag onto the counter.
The overripe doze, the dream

beneath its skin: the sun. And not just that,
but the meat, the possibility

of light and glisten. Softening,

and sweet, the melon at rest
like a boy's dreaming head, like a shelter,

a house that is not a ruin yet, but will be

someday, or a boy asleep on the sofa,
the boy dreaming that now,

now the roof's caved in. Now the termites
are in the woodwork, now the house

is a shudder on stilts, now the water
is rolling, is rotting them away.

The melon, asleep as it always is,
the house crumbling to its knees on the beach

and the boy awash inside, knowing
some time, soon, yes,

knowing the light will find him here,

in the clasp of it, the cup

of the palms of his hands that open,

unstoppably, like a melon opens,
into a second age.

How They Survive   by Susan Terris

On the broad Shamali Plains,
In the desolate village of Qhurqul

The enemy has cut down grape vines, walnut
And mulberry trees, felled the apple orchards.
And Amir? He has returned to a well
Dammed with rocks,
A house turned to rubble by mortar fire.
What has he salvaged? A tin box, a chair,
A tub without a bottom.
Now, in the char of the old kitchen,
He and his family camp out.
They have no grapes, no nuts or bright berries,
No apples to eat, but they do keep warm
Slowly burning what they have lost.

Family Portrait   by Susan Terris

Avocado

Alligator pear, Mother calls it. Let it ripen
slowly on the tree, then on the windowsill.
A rough beauty, yet inside — greasy and salty-sweet.

Bananas

Brother and I, Chiquita stickers on our foreheads,
spurn rumors of tarantulas lurking in the bunch.
If they're too ripe, we mash them for spider bread.

Cucumbers

Warty green fingers in a crate from Sansones, washed,
then steamed with garlic, dill, and kosher salt.
Father says deli pickles are better than ones we put up.

Doughnuts

Brother and I mix the batter, cut it into floured rings,
and Mother floats them in the deep fryer,
treats to fatten neighbor kids, Vicki and Johnny.

Eggplant

Satin-sheen purple, the color makes my mouth water.
But Mother peels and cuts it into white rounds
and fries it (for Father) to an offensive yellow mush.

Frankfurters

Ours come from a take-a-number deli. Wait your turn.
Make Brother ask. Boil them up and serve
on rye. *Don't pick out the caraway seeds*, Mother says.

Grapefruit

Cut in half — two shiny cartwheels. Use a special
knife to loosen up the wedges. Father and
Mother don't use sugar. They sprinkle it with salt.

Hash

Not in our house. Father doesn't like food in his food,
so Mother serves one meat, one starch, one
       vegetable: brown, white, green — to look good on a plate.

Ice Cream

Father walks us to buy vanilla, strawberry, chocolate,
and we come home with dripping cartons. Mother
refreezes it in ice trays to a cold, tooth-aching crunch.

Juice

Every morning, Mother fixes Father's fresh O.J. ,
and he drinks the pulpy stuff before he takes
his ice water, his coffee, his hot toast with hard butter.

Kraut

It's cabbage, of course, sliced thin, transparent, soured.
Mother serves it with the fat orange franks.
Then, for years, she keeps the leftovers on the icebox shelf.

Lemons

Good with fillet of sole, Father says, but when we
squeeze them, seeds fall out. For our curbside
business, Brother and I make a sour, seedy lemonade.

Milk

We're already big, so Mother never forces us to drink it.
But she feeds Sister— our new baby
with thin white stuff that dribbles from her breasts.

Noodles

Brother and I eat them buttered with brisket.
When they slip and hang off our forks,
Father frowns, and Mother says, *Children, don't slurp*.

Oatmeal

Better than Cream of Wheat, especially with milk,
raisins, and banana. But Brother and Sister
don't like lumps, so when I sleep at Vicki's, I ask for it.

Peas

Tiny green ones out of cans, and Mother serves them
too much. Sister squashes them with her fingers
while Brother and I hide them under lamb chop bones.

Quince

We pick them to make jelly by dripping bloody juice
through cheesecloth hung from cabinet handles.
Welch's Grape is better, Father says, spreading it on toast.

Roast Beef

Father's favorite—always called Rare Roast Beef,
though he likes the end. Mother uses Lawry's Salt,
and lets Brother eat just the heart so fat won't touch his lips.

Sugar/Salt

We cook with both. Sometimes Sister spoons sugar
on thick-buttered Wonder Bread, but in our family
we prefer salt or spice to anything (even chocolate) sweet.

Tomatoes

Every day Father says, *Tomatoes... are the spice of life.*
We grow them on hairy vines, help Mother stew
and can them for the cellar, but Father only eats them fresh.

Upsidedown Cake

Rings of canned pineapple and maraschinos.
When company comes, Sister and I help Mother
bake it, but the cake looks much better than it tastes.

Vegetable Soup

Father's other favorite— soup isn't food, it's soup—
with beef bone and barley and leftover peas.
Cooking, summer or winter, and Mother serves it nightly.

Watermelon

Mother thumps it hard at Sansones. At home, Father
cuts it on the picnic table. *Another spice of life,* he says,
as we hold dripping wedges and spit seeds at one another.

XXX

If the soup pot is empty, we have Campbell's Alphabet
where the xxx-es can't be used for that forbidden word,
so we put them on our spoons and feed each other slimy kisses.

Yesterdays

1978: eight thousand days ago—Father died. Yet Mother,
now a soft voice on the line, goes on, still talks of food,
her tone growing fainter. Like Brother's voice. Like Sister's.

Zest

Grate only the zest—the yellow part, Mother says, *because
the skin below is bitter.* Careless, I grate lemon and
my fingertips. In pain, I think: sunshine and I think: blood.

Woolgathering   **by Susan McGowan**

When Mama smacked my face
for eyeing boys in church,
I thought of how she slaps dough
on the floured hickory slab grandpa
shaved off the big tree out back. Mama
digs her palm into a lump of bread
and flips it back onto the table, where
it wobbles under her hand, like a water balloon,

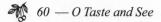

and the yeast smells same as sweat
that dripped down the broad-faced boy,
munching on a daffodil tip as I slipped
the heel of my hand along his carved hip.
I think Mama could smell that rising, too:
her second slap rang sharper than the first.

Blood Oranges   **by Sarah Kennedy**

We're passing the Mason jar, straight
from Franklin County, where our students'
parents keep their stills. Everyone's crocked

by midnight, slumming after a dinner
of salmon and cucumber sauce, a good bottle
of Pinot Blanc, but it's early yet for English

profs, drunk and cracking jokes
about Virginia hicks and their sheep.
They all love my sterling, my antique

Dresden, and I'm almost bombed enough
to tell, as though it were just any country story,
about a boy, crouched beneath a manger,

eye against a rat-hole while his old man
helped a stallion onto the mare. Back
in the Midwestern fifties, he slept with his father,

sister snugged in with their mother. Later,
in the army, he would hate the gnarled hands
curled into the fence at Fort Sill, the familiar

voice wailing, *Send my boy home.* I know
I would never confess that, after
our wedding, he wanted to spill it all: how

he came back to work the land, laying hands—

he couldn't stop—on young girls, horses,
and, yes, the ewes. Even long divorced,
I'm silent. They could never forgive
such a revelation; how could they bear
to know me tomorrow morning? But

the marriage was real as my brother's eyes
glaring across my girlhood bed, my dad's
boozy wooing of his daughters, all

those home-grown horrors. Somebody laughs
that a kid we've struggled through freshman comp
will flunk out and marry his mother. Everyone roars.

The Dickey quotations fly. *Every field is as dark
as that barn*, my husband once said and I pretended
not to hear. Even now, I can fake it, turning

to our dessert: I've split the skin of an elegant brie
and slit the flesh—bright for contrast, arranged
to shock in a porcelain bowl—of blood oranges.

The Cake   by Stuart Lishan

Out of ache, egging on a hard
"C" unsoftened, fastened to ground wheat,
four fingers' worth of sugar, chocolate, rind
of orange peel, comes slice. Not the verb, which
does damage, but the noun, which gives palm full,
fist worth, a heft of hand through which you taste.
Now to eat, bordering on dig, a forked
backhoe bucket dip drawn in. First cake frost,
textured of snow crust. Below it your tongue
burrows like a worm where it is less sweet.
This is what you eat, as you stare beyond
what you know, up at your father staring
at the object of his forked pricking. The stain
of what you've eaten settles about your mouth

like a bathtub ring. Now your milk spills, your plate
like a freshet fouled with brown bilge. Now
a slap and sting of hand strike, of squelched
cry, of "Clean it up. Now, stupid,
I said now."
                    How the act of such eating bred
silence, rising in a yeast of forks
tinking on plates about a table, a loaf
of unspeak, followed by a scrape of kitchen
chair on faded linoleum, a standing
up, a walking out, leaving behind
a tired-eyed woman tied with apron,
two young children, a cake, the memory
of rising from such batter.

The Weight of Sweetness   by Li-Young Lee

No easy thing to bear, the weight of sweetness.

Song, wisdom, sadness, joy: sweetness
equals three of any of these gravities.

See a peach bend
the branch and strain the stem until
it snaps.
Hold the peach, try the weight, sweetness
and death so round and snug
in your palm.
And, so, there is
the weight of memory:

Windblown, a rain-soaked
bough shakes, showering
the man and the boy.
They shiver in delight,
and the father lifts from his son's cheek
one green leaf
fallen like a kiss.
The good boy hugs a bag of peaches

his father has entrusted
to him.
Now he follows
his father, who carries a bagful in each arm.
See the look on the boy's face
as his father moves
faster and farther ahead, while his own steps
flag, and his arms grow weak, as he labors
under the weight
of peaches.

Fever Bouquet   by Wendy Bishop

I'm defrosting the last of last summer's pesto—
homegrown basil and Romano cheese,
garlic with Georgia pecans—watching
Florida light flood a February evening
while my daughter's fever spikes, 103 degrees
and worrisome. She says "Oh god it hurts"
with a too quiet, twelve-year-old's-voice.
I place the cold washcloth at her forehead,
raise her shirt to check the rash. Her breast buds
slow me; I was thinking of other things.
A small shock, though we've been expecting
them together for months and weeks.
She sighs with her croupy chest and turns
in her body heat, slipping back toward childhood,
labored heartbeats held between lush, chapping lips.
Two days until Valentines and all the valentines
I collected in the past could dance on the head
of a pin for what they have taught me about how
to help with the betwixt and betweens—the almost
grown up, the almost well, the not quite but soon-to-be
springs. The freezer finally is empty. Outside, brown
winter grass waits to serve up its latent seeds.
I drop capellini into boiling water. A room away,
her breath evens and she sleeps. I sniff
green and garlic, pour heart-red wine. I eat. \

Vending Machine   by Grey Held

Let me do It!, he shouts.
I take the coins from my pocket,
and he counts out the quarters—*three, four.*
I pick him up so he can slide
the money in. He pushes the buttons:
K—I whisper.
10—I whisper. Out falls
the package of peanut butter crackers.
He grabs it from me, yanks
the little red string that opens the wrapper
and it falls to the floor. He unglues
the top half of a sandwich,
scrapes the peanut butter off
with his teeth, his tongue, polishing
the cracker into the soggy circle
he hands to me. *Your half,* he says,
and I take it.

My Mother and the Bums   by Grace Butcher

Thirty years later I sit on the same porch
of the same house where I seem to have always lived,
the same porch where the bums sat,
the hobos who wandered our road then
and came here always in the sun it seemed,
came to the door and said Please M'am
and my mother said Sit down and wait
and I will get you something.
I always peered through the window,
afraid they'd see me,
but my mother just cooked them eggs and bacon,
made toast and coffee, gave them 50 cents.
Their whiskery faces. Their dirty hands.
The shabby coats. The plates they had eaten from.
The plates coming back into our clean kitchen

and the men, looking old, shambling on down our road.
It always seemed to be summer;
they moved in a blue and gold brightness
in their dirty clothes and their awful shoes.

My mother is dead ten years. No hobo
has come here for at least that long.
Where have they gone and why did they come?
This porch. The food. And fifty cents.
I guess my mother wasn't afraid.
Feeding bums was something you did then.
I wish I had known how to love my mother.
She didn't mind the whiskery faces at the door
or washing the plates they had eaten from.
I sit here on the same porch where they sat.
My mother gives *me* something now,
even though it's too late.

Thirteen   by Susan Grimm

No fireflies. It's not dusk.
No play with early and late.
The only threshold here is the screen door,
wooden, the tight coil of wire
that closes and closes.

She stands by the screen door in the shadow
of the porch. The house seems full
of purpose. Inside the women
drink coffee, the grit of raspberry
pie in their teeth.

This is not about containment although
there's more jostle and spread outside,
although the women drink things
disguised of their bitterness.

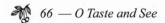

It's time she chooses the hard thing,
the ugly thing, the shape of a certain
age, though we may whoop and moan, still,
inside. The round plates, the cut pieces
of pie like tongues mimic our sound.

My daughter reaches for the hot, dark
cup and a place at the table.

At Ninety-Eight   **by Lynn Powell**

> I sure as hell hope the Lord's got beans
> to break and string in heaven.
>   —Aunt Roxy

Her mind goes blank
imagining what pearly gates
and boulevards of gold—what
contraption of an afterlife—
could matter more than sweet
potatoes garden dug, still damp,
a green bonfire of mustards,
the pumpkin fattening like a golden calf.
She's lost patience
with that infernal flirt, the future,
outlived the widowed longings of the past.

And though I needle her to tell me
who 80 years ago she loved,
who 60 years ago she nursed,
her loss has turned as silver
and familiar as the moon.
She'd rather go buy nlyons at the 5 & 10,
then, holding to me like a lover,
try on her bright new lipstick, red as fruit.

garden

The Blackberry Thicket   by Ann Stanford

I stand here in the ditch, my feet on a rock in the water,
Head-deep in a coppice of thorns,
Picking wild blackberries,
Watching the juice-dark rivulet run
Over my fingers, marking the lines and whorls,
Remembering stains—
The blue of mulberry on the tongue
Brown fingers after walnut husking,
And the green smudge of grass—
The earnest part
Of heat and orchards and sweet springing places.
Here I am printed with the earth
Always and always the earth ground into the fingers,
And the arm scratched in thickets of spiders.
Over the marshy water the cicada rustles,
A runner snaps sharp into place.
The dry leaves are a presence,
A companion that follows up under the trees of the orchard
Repeating my footsteps. I stop to listen.
Surely not alone
I stand in this quiet in the shadow
Under a roof of bees.

The Beekeeper   by Steve Wilson
— Adlesic, Slovenia

Summer comes luscious as amber and honey.

It flows up from willow roots, the rushes' dead stalks –
a hum soft under sound – to whisper the fields awake.
It floats within wind-rivers shaped from prairie grasses.

Borne upon bees' wings, the days are sweetened to fullness.
Suddenly, in the orchard the greenest suggestions – new
leaves – try the light, urging the trees' black branches.

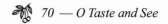

No surprise, then, to see bees leave their hives. They'll linger
and linger along the white of pear blossoms: a white, perfumed,
that through the village goes, quick with warmth,

even down to the stilled, chill shadows of the forest.

Learning to Clam   **by Don Bogen**

On the cold coast west out of Hoquiam,
I'm a stalker with a short-handled gun,
looking for dimples in damp sand to scoop out
and slosh in. Clamming is watching,
your close friend said, as we raced here under
a rising fog. But my own clam-eye's
unfocused like a baby's, and the dawn-gray beach
gets littered with caved-in holes until
I learn to see under sand.
                        That strange tug
of life and then release as the numb hand
pulls the razored shell though a suck of mud,
after three hours it almost becomes
familiar. The backs of my shoulders remember
the bite of that bent-up shovel, my palms
are marked with the grain of its handle.
The gritty catch clatters in our bags
all the long way back.
                        In the barnlike
kitchen we learn to slice off guts, wash
the ribbony innards in the sink. A bucket
fills with brittle hunks of shell, clean parts
plop in a mixing bowl. Dipped in flour now,
the milk-colored meat is turning gold in oil.
I catch a whiff of ocean off the pan. Clam
steam fogs up all the windows, enclosing us
like memory.

Picking Blackberries with a Friend   **by Robert Hass**
Who Has Been Reading Jacques Lacan

August is dust here. Drought
stuns the road,
but juice gathers in the berries.

We pick them in the hot
slow-motion of midmorning.
Charlie is exclaiming:

for him it is twenty years ago
and raspberries and Vermont.
We have stopped talking

about *L'Histoire de la vérité*,
about subject and object
and the mediation of desire.

Our ears are stoppered
in the bee-hum. And Charlie,
laughing wonderfully,

beard stained purple
by the word *juice*,
goes to get a bigger pot.

The Story of Butter   **by Deanna Pickard**

Lent out summers to her aunt's farm,
small, she had to stretch to churn the butter.
Wagon wheels beat the poor dust and settled
on the windowsills and the sorry coat
of the only cow. Her wise cousins held

yellow-capped dandelions under her chin
and proved to her, her love of butter.

They knew the secrets of the dark bull
and the heavy mare, and the dizzying smoke
from catalpa cigars they would light up

behind the bank barn. She never learned
to like the smoke but butter had not lost
its pleasure. Though these last years,
she couldn't remember how it came to be
in her kitchen or where she would find it.

Now her daughter intrudes on Mondays,
not asking but arriving with yellow pail,
soaps, and energy that makes her swimmy-headed.
A whirlwind beats the cushions around her
and teeters her noon naps. This girl,

who wears her late husband's disposition,
holds no cream in her bucket. Instead
she puts the dog out, and counts the quarters
of delivered butter from the corner grocery,
shaking her head. On those days,

the old woman refuses to hear. And when
the full plate is set like a clock before her,
she moves the food round and round and eats
only bread, smeared with a taste of butter.

Watering the Sheep   **by John Hershman**

    after Basho

An old frog
Jumps into the sky—
Splash!

Dark Navajo boy
Sitting under evergreens
Eating hard frybread.

A roadrunner, big
As a chicken strikes the pond—
Swallowing wet jade.

Sheep and goats nibble
Sweet grass at the water's edge,
The sheep dog laps blue.

The horned toad's eyes
Oblivious to the light
Waits for a buzzing.

The lightning bird skips
Over the toad, over the boy's
Foot, into the pines.

Heat waves hang above—
The tree's shade is even hot,
His lips are sand dunes.

Another frog jumps—
The sheep move onto ripe reeds
Chewing and splashing.

* * *

Grandma kneads a cloud
She lets it rise, heats a pan—
Bread waits for her sheep.

Moving, 1880 by Kathrine Varnes

When they would move out West, the men went first.

Great grandma Jessie's dad and uncle left
to find a place to live. The women waited
for almost a year and then they heard
that they had land in Idaho. They packed
up what they could—Jessie was almost two
so she could help some—wrapped up the brand new baby
(that would be Grammy's cousin, your great great cousin,
Olivia) and took the train past towns

and fields and desert. She tried counting cows
then horses, sheep then people at train stops, but it all
went by too fast. Then it got dark outside
and the train seemed louder going past places
she might never see, and people kept walking through
the passage. Her mom told her *Go to sleep*
but she was too excited to.
She closed her eyes but through the night her mom

and aunt were up rustling and whispering
about the baby. She was much too quiet,
so pale they thought she might not make the trip.
So Jessie lay there in the dark and watched
them pass the baby back and forth until
the morning came and she was still alive.
When the train reached their stop, they were so glad
to step out on the platform. It was summer,

hot and dry and bright. The men were there
and everyone was looking at the baby.
Then Jessie's dad picked her up and they were all
together. Her uncle held a paper bag,
and he pulled out an orange fruit, round
and furry, which he rubbed some as he passed
them around and they bit through the pretty skin
to reach the sweetness all at once

and Gramma Jessie said it was like eating
flowers. Someone had planted trees out there.
And that was her first peach. In Idaho.

Hunting Wild Mushrooms   **by Julia Levine**

When he tracks the wild spores,
Probing the underside of oak
For orange trumpets of Chanterelle
Or the inky blush of Bluetts,
Centuries of mycelium strands
Threading the forest floor, waiting for weather
To lift the fruiting bodies out of blackness,

I think of what sliver of chance opened
In the years before war,
His parents crossing the Atlantic with linens
And the wedding pictures where they sit
On a narrow bench among ghosts:
Stern aunts, a blonde child straddling shoulders,
Young men still flush with dance and vodka,
Entire families about to button up those dark coats
Of earth, the soldiers' rifles insistent
That they dig their own graves
By handfuls, a village of bodies
Sinking under the forest's dense litter;
So that now, when he kneels in the graying canopy
Exhuming Amanitas, I see his hands
As prayer, how they reveal to light
What waits to be remembered,
Their search
For what returns from that damp quiet.

Winter Nightfall   **by Wendell Berry**

The fowls speak and sing, settling for the night.
The mare shifts in the bedding.
In her womb her foal sleeps and grows,
within and within and within. Her jaw grinds,
meditative in the fragrance of timothy.
Soon now my own rest will come.
The silent river flows on in the dusk, miles and miles.
Outside the walls and on the roof and in the woods
the cold rain falls.

February 2, 1968   **by Wendell Berry**

In the dark of the moon, in flying snow, in the dead of winter,
war spreading, families dying, the world in danger,
I walk the rocky hillside, sowing clover.

Nectar   **by Ann Townsend**

I am sucking a lime popsicle
and pruning my roses; hands full
of the aspects of summer, I don't see
the bee light until too late
and it's at my tongue, little thistle
of wings and a poison dart. But
my daughter's cried out *bumblebee*
and I spit in time—the bee, wet,
frazzled, or merely interrupted,
fumbles into purple statice.
The bees are unfashioning the flowers,
dozens softly humming and oblivious
to human near-disaster. I am dizzy
from bending too long,

from sudden rising and a surge
of adrenaline, the blank
and vivid sun on my face. But
there is no fragility like the flowers,
that can be cut down with a twist
of the secateurs' sharp blade, so
we press on. We carry the severed
stems to the woods, fodder for the spring
garden, and the bees still work the blossoms
clinging as they dry in our arms.

Murder in the Good Land   by Patiann Rogers

      Murder among the creek narrows
and shafts of rice grass, among lacy
coverlets and field sacks, among basement
apple barrels and cellar staples
of onion and beet;
                beneath piled stones,
razed, broken and scattered stones,
beneath cow bridges, draw bridges, T girders
crossed, and cables, beneath brome, spadefoot,
beneath roots of three-awn
                    and heaven; murder
in the sky between stalks of spikesedge,
between harrier and wolf willow, between
the bedroom walls of formidable sluts
and saints, in the sad blindnesses
of moon and mole, in light as curt
and clearcut as blades of frost
magnified;
            through blanks of winter wind
through summer soapweed, through welcoming
gates and bolted gates, throughout the blood-rushing
grief of the swarmy sea;
                murder beside gods
down heathen colonnades, down corridors of scholars
and beggars, down the cathedral colonnades

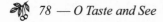

of orchards in harvest;
               murder with the clench
of white clover, with the slip of the wandering
tattler, with the slow splash of window
curtains flowing inward
                 with morning air; murder
in the winsome, murder in the wayward,
murder in canyon wrens, in the low beating bell
in the womb, in bone rafters,
                  in mushroom
rings and rosy rings; murder, murder,
murder immortal, pervasive, supreme
everywhere in the good land.

Bearded Barley   **by Allen Braden**

Proud and skinny tow-head
stretching for sunshine,

slender arrow of gold
or wand with stiff whiskers,

you offer us summer magic
out of water, dirt and light.

The millstone, the baker,
the slave, pulpit and priest,

they all send their regards.
You send back your straw

so they may build empires
and pray for your safe-keeping
when a cloudburst in August
bows you flat against the earth

below the teeth of the combine,
even the sickle's blade and cradle;

or when a twister drives you
clear through a telephone pole;

when the unbelievable seems true.
I could have sworn I saw you

hopping a train for the mill,
determined on being refined

into a loaf of bread or angel food
or maybe the body of Christ.

The Little Permanence   **by Imogene Bolls**

At the morning window you see
for the first time the garden
for what it *really* is—not survival
and beans in February—but a transitory haven
for vegetables, flowers, birds, your eyes.

Bean leaves past their prime
are yellow and curling, late pods
now husky brown throats of themselves.
Broccoli, grown gangly, towers above
the rest, gone to bloom and butterfly,
seed and worm. Even so, tomatoes
ripen like joyful, bursting hearts
waiting to be stolen. Robins and jays
are waiting to steal. The mums beam—
round and golden—in a corner, and
the red and green caladium is doing well.

Celery, carrots, squash—you are struck
by the little permanence of what you thought
you had preserved for freezer and stomach,
by how, even now, enzymes and hoarfrost

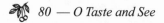

are at permanent work on the temporary,

by how, fenced and private, the garden
for one summer of one yard
is another kind of nourishment
than you had intended to plant.

A crimson-breasted finch drops,
soundless, into green like a throb
of blood, a heartbeat past as it is
felt, lost as it is found.

The Recluse Works in Her Country Garden   by Grace Butcher

In my country garden
I murmur to myself,
let all my thoughts be words
and try them out aloud
with no one there to see my lips moving.
I can address the trees, the blades of grass,
the weeds, the empty rows to tell them
what will come, the soil itself that
crumbles in my hands.

The wind answers, translated by the spruce
and cedars I can still remember as being small.
Have I always spoken my thoughts out loud?
When did that start?

As in a movie when the camera pans away
and up into the sky, I imagine being seen
only by someone too far away to matter:
I would be a speck here in this
warm, dark soil, barely more than
part of the whole earth, the garden
edging into pasture, pasture into woods,
all my words unseen, nothing I do here

noticed, time of no consequence
except in the swing of seasons,

and I am always the same age: somewhere
in the middle of my life, always alone
except for the company of vegetables,
coming and going in their quiet brilliance,
some living half underground, no one
really knowing what they are doing
under there

until there comes a time of sudden need
and they go gladly to that hand
that pulls them free, that knows
exactly what it wants,
and takes it.
They go gladly then.

A Display of Mackerel   by Mark Doty

They lie in parallel rows,
on ice, head to tail,
each a foot of luminosity

barred with black bands,
which divide the scales'
radiant sections

like seams of lead
in a Tiffany window.
Iridescent, watery

prismatics: think abalone,
the wildly rainbowed
mirror of a soapbubble sphere,

think sun on gasoline.
Splendor, and splendor,

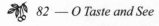

and not a one in any way

distinguished from the other
—nothing about them
of individuality. Instead

they're *all* exact expressions
of the one soul,
each a perfect fulfillment

of heaven's template,
mackerel essence. As if,
after a lifetime arriving

at this enameling, the jeweler's
made uncountable examples,
each as intricate

in its oily fabulation
as the one before.
Suppose we could iridesce,

like these, and lose ourselves
entirely in the universe
of shimmer—would you want
to be yourself only,
unduplicatable, doomed
to be lost? They'd prefer,

plainly, to be flashing participants,
multitudinous. Even now
they seem to be bolting

forward, heedless of stasis.
They don't care they're dead
and nearly frozen,

just as, presumably,
they didn't care that they were living:
all, all for all,

the rainbowed school
and its acres of brilliant classrooms,
in which no verb is singular,

or every one is. How happy they seem,
even on ice, to be together, selfless,
which is the price of gleaming.

Peanut Lockerby   by Linda Kittell

Berger, Manzer, Junebug and me
bucked the hay, first crop to last, most years
a good three cuttings. July
was warm enough for the sweet
sour taste of ginger water, jugs wrapped
tight in burlap to keep them cool. Early August, the beer
slid down easy, my skin prickling like in mid-
September when my self, all chaff and long hours,
grabbed hay hooks and gloves. That last hay
was the best—us against the weather, us against ourselves—
watching the sky gray
to the color of a junco's back. Me trying to beat
the rain, Junebug working
against God Almighty.
On the last truck, we'd lay down, roll and tip
on top of the load and over
the fields toward home.
Inside, Sabra had baked all day—her biscuits
and ham gravy, three kinds
of potato, macaroni, bowls thick
with butter, the pot roasts and lima beans,
pies and ice cream. Outside
the first fall rain soaked
the last petunias
that bloomed along her sills.

stories

Two Lives: Making Supper at Lake George by F. Richard Thomas

In suspenders, white silk shirt, sleeves rolled, black bow tie,
Stieglitz cuts onions at the kitchen sink,
lays the purple skins on a cotton towel,
a tear runs into his mustache.
Setting the table, O'Keeffe carries plates and silver graciously,
                              crooking her long fingers ostentatiously.
Her green muslin dress falls from one shoulder.
Her neck is strong.
She dreams of the sun-bleached skulls of horses.
He sees the dark pools of Dorothy's eyes.

A sudden gust and a boom of thunder
          lift the lace curtain like a veil and snuff the white candle on the
          table.
Alfred raises his eyes from the onions, out the kitchen window, to the
boiling sky.
Georgia looks up from placing a fork, out the dining room window, across
          the yard;
          she sees the gray slate of the lake glazed at the base of the hills like
          the shining silver knife in her hand.
As the rain plops, a breath of ozone, wet wool, and sweet grass
          sprays through the window screens.
Spring, the skin's thrill, breaks into goose bumps on their bare arms
          and their nostrils swell with the fragrance of God.
The canvas edge of her calla lily flutters like a hummingbird on the easel.
His cloud photos on the coffee table billow and slide and rest again in
          disarray.
The book on the floor flips through many chapters.
A thin line of smoke streams from the candle.
In this light the wine is dark as blood in the two glasses on the dining room
          table.

Georgia lifts her shoulders together and her dress falls to the floor.
Alfred slips quickly and carefully from his clothes,

          draping them over a dining room chair.
She folds her easel and takes up her palette;
he fetches his camera from the coffee table

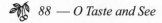

and they walk into the rain,

separately.
They do not look at each other for fear of bursting into flame.
The screen door bangs twice,

> then taps

and murmurs on its hinges
in the storm.

My Mother Paints Again   by Jonathan Andersen

Her first attempt in decades —
a gift for my wife and me —
a watercolor, still-life
hangs in our kitchen:

three ears of corn in a basket,
two husks torn back, revealing
milky, plump kernels.

I grieve
> for so much left unpainted:

rudbeccia, tall and stalky, spreading
and blooming up out of hard pack gravel driveway—
oranges, yellows, reds
> as varied and flickering in the wind
  as flame.

Or the sudden face of a lynx
> perched in the mist on an old stone wall
in the twisting, early morning farm road drive to

the small red brick school where she cooked hot meals for years

and watched over children who needed her, like
pink-cheeked second grader Mary Coombs,
whose love

was not quite yet snuffed out by the dazed mommy that
filled her moldy thermos with beer.

Or abstract-expressionist works:
        audacious strokes of violent
                black against radiant schemes and looping green
swirls with titles like "Self-Portrait: Sis, 1962" or
"Divorce After Three Decades: Three Weeks In."

And mixed-media pieces in cardboard, canvas, old
utensils and electric light. Anything. But mostly
anything with hope, anything that assumes a future,
or reminds us that grief
        is an easy posture, a slippery emotion,

not worthy of this work that hangs in my kitchen, this still-
life that moves with butter melting in summer heat and
crooked, old-fashioned rows of bursting kernels—
some for food, some for seed, enough to live on not just today
but also tomorrow.

Reading Hemingway   **by James Cummins**

Reading Hemingway makes me so hungry,
for *jambon*, cheeses, and a dry white wine.
Cold, of course, very cold. And very dry.

Reading Hemingway makes some folks angry:
the hip drinking, the bitter pantomime.
But reading Hemingway makes me hungry

for the good life, the sun, the fish, the sky:
blue air, *white water*, dinner on the line...
Had it down cold, he did. And dry. Real dry.

But Papa had it all, the *brio*, the *Brie*:
clear-eyed, tight-lipped, advancing on a *stein*...
Reading Hemingway makes me so hungry,

I'd knock down Monsieur Stevens, too, if I
drank too much *retsina* before we dined.
(Too old, that man, and way too cold. And dry

enough to rub one's famished nerves awry,
kept talking past the kitchen's closing time!)
Reading Hemingway makes me so hungry...
And cold, of course. So cold. And very dry.

Breakfast at Keseberg's Diner   by Kay Sloan

Sacramento, 1848

After the snow, after carved corpses
exposed the icy survival of the last
  Donner Party members, the Belgian
Keseberg boasted of eating the frozen flesh
  of dead companions, starved pioneers
who'd stormed the Great Salt desert in five frantic
  days, depleted of water, oxen
fleeing, only to face the High Sierras'
  great face, a road no wagon could pass.
They made it a day late, double-teamed, double-
  crossed by a scheming guide trying to
cross that high pass before the first blizzard struck.
  A day too late. They arrived the night
the snows began, flurries flying random as
  luck. Inside lean-tos and sheds, the log
shanties with beds of straw and animal fur,
  the watch began: the slow erosion
of food supplies, of skin that shrank on faces
  till masks of hunger hid all but the eyes.

The angel and the animal breathed
together in bodies hungry for each death,
  the next feast that would mean survival.
They carefully labeled the muscles, organs:
  kin would never eat kin. Though they kept
certain taboos, their two Indian guides crept
  off into the forest, horrified,
to die alone. Later, after rescuers
  brought the last survivors to safety
(*How can we call ourselves decent, if we fail*
  to go? they'd asked from their valley fort.
We must do it for California's good name),
  after Keseberg had forgotten
the cold and wind and endless white days buried
  at that forsaken camp, he answered
when they asked what it's like to eat human flesh.
  Smiling, he confessed: when the body
craves only life, the taste is not so bad. Ghoul,
  they called him, thrilled to look in his eyes
and say they would never have done as he did,
  rather die than pick meat from a corpse.

When he opened his breakfast diner
in Sacramento, they stood in lines outside
  to wait. Keseberg had hung pictures
above the door: the High Sierras' beauty.
  In the morning, the customers came,
ordering ham and pancakes, watching the man
  or savage at his stove, with their eyes
curious as a cat's, wondering what pact
  had been made between angel and beast,
words written in blood that might season a feast.

Revelation: Theresienstadt Story   by William Heynan

One June day, 1943,
Eva Roubickova, prisoner,
tended sheep on a slope
where there was a cherry tree
with "marvelous red cherries,"
as she writes in her diary.
She & the three others with her
kept watch as they ate the cherries,
which were not quite ripe.
Then she was standing there
with a branch in her hand
when *crack*! the whole branch
broke off. Of course,
at that moment an SS appeared.
Sabotage twice over, he said,
to eat cherries & to break the tree.
He picked up the branch,
handed it to her: "Here,
take the rest of the fruit."

We expected a beating, torture,
her death on the spot
or at Auschwitz after transport,
but the SS said,
"If someone else had discovered you,
imagine what had become of you.
You're visible from far away.
For all I care, break off
as many branches as you like,
but don't let people see you."
The women started to cry,
relieved, touched that an SS
could still be kind.
"Even among Germans,
there are still humans," she writes.
That night, despite
diarrhea & stomach ache,
she thanked God
for that food on his hillside.

La Monstrua Vestida, La Monstrua Desnuda   **by Myrna Stone**

after two portraits by Juan Carreño De Miranda, 1680-86

"Eugenia...at the age of six, already weighing more than
130 pounds...was brought to Madrid to be exhibited as a freak."

Great Masters of European Painting

She is all done up
in red and white, with bows in her hair
    and bows at her shoulders,

the tangible weight
of her brocade gown, the excessive flesh
    beneath it, grounding us

in this painterly moment,
a graceless lull in which she regards us
    with undisguised

disdain. In her own future
she will greet the few men who come to her
    bed with just this jaundiced

expression, invoking
in them, as she invokes in us, little civility.
    But, in the here and now,

she is a dwarf-child
holding an apple in each hand, a curiosity
    taken from the village

of Bárcenas and bound
to the court of Charles the Second, posing
    at his command, clothed

or unctuously unclothed,
a leafy vine wreath ornamenting her head,
    her gaze directed away

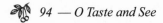

from the sweetmeats on Carreño
De Miranda's platter—his bribery of fruits,
   sugared hazelnuts and jellies,

of candied rose petals—
succulents of such exuberance, such gloss
   and weave, that even she,

Eugenia Martínez Vallejo,
might see in them a virtue beyond gustation.
   And here, too, is perversity:

that in this house of plenty,
this province of fish and fowl, ox and lamb,
   it is her mother's round cakes

of unleavened wheat and rye—
coarse and dense as cobbles—for which
   she says she hungers.

The Harvesters   **by Myrna Stone**
   oil on wood, 1565

Here, Bruegel offers us
   grain as allegory, as a rich
bullion load of light under
   a sapphirine, Netherlandish sky,

his clever coruscation
   he sets burning on hillsides
above Brussels, in standing
   shocks and a mountainous stack

aloft on an ox-drawn cart
   in the distance of a grassy
lane. Even the wry faces
   of his peasants—those wielding

scythes or sickles,
    those eating and drinking
beneath the umber limbs
    of an alder—reflect its wheaty

luster, sheen he repeats
    on a wickerwork basket
and the bean-shaped loaf
    a woman is lifting and slicing.

And here, too, he implies
    the fecund action of the berry,
bucolic, sexual, its robust
    addle of endosperm, bran, germ,

and all we can imagine
    of the uses to which he put it—
porridge in a bowl, bread
    on a plate with its dollop of jam

or honey, a belly full
    of ambition—and always sun
coming up and going down
    into it so that the heat might last.

The Spoon   by Charles Simic

An old spoon
Bent, gouged,
Polished to an evil
Glitter.

It has bitten
Into my life—
This kennel-bone
Sucked thin.

Now, it is a living
Thing: ready

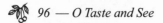

To scratch a name
On a prison wall—

Ready to be passed on
To the little one
Just barely
Beginning to walk.

Fork   **by Charles Simic**

This strange thing must have crept
Right out of hell.
It resembles a bird's foot
Worn around the cannibal's neck.

As you hold it in your hand,
As you stab with it into a piece of meat,
It is possible to imagine the rest of the bird:
Its head which like your fist
Is large, bald, beakless and blind.

Haiku & Senryu   **by Yvonne Hardenbrook**

lunch break
hardhat astride the brick wall
peeling an egg

deep bowl
the cat flattens his ears
to the milk

iced tea —
a higher pitched clink
with each sip

beach picnic —
leftovers taking off
in the pelican

on my doorstep
a basket of zucchini —
his quick getaway

fast food line
someone behind me ordering —
his cellular phone

Who Made Such Good Pies   by Jim Heynan

It was always good to visit that lady because she made such good pies.
What was so good about them was the little waves on the edge of the
crusts. The boys could tell how big a piece they were getting by count-
ing those little waves. A piece of her pie looked like this.

perfect little waves

Eight waves was a big piece.
   How does she do it? the other ladies asked. No one knew.
   The boys walked over to her house early one day before everyone was
going over there for pie. They stood outside her kitchen window and
watched her making her pies. This is what they saw.
   When the lady had the pie crust rolled out in the pie pan, she reached
into her mouth and pulled out her false teeth. Then she took them and
pushed them down on the pie crust all the way around. The spaces
between her false teeth made all those nice little waves that everybody
liked so much.
   Pretty soon everyone came for fresh pie.
   What beautiful pies! all the ladies said.
   The boys got eight-wave pieces that day.
   Every now and then, between bites of that good pie, the boys looked at
the lady. She was watching everyone eat and grinning a big grin.

Sharif's Fish Stew

by David Hassler

The smell of fish floats
under the crack of my door.
Sharif is cooking his weekly stew.
He carries the scent of his spices
in his hands and hair, and they
will not leave the soles of his feet,
though he washes them before prayer.
I believe his stew makes him strong.
Perhaps Muhammed can smell
the faith of his followers.

Sharif, my friend, keeps his faith
on the roof of our boarding house,
where he rents a tin shack that rattles
in the rain. He prays there at dawn
before riding the trains two hours
outside of the city to work in a factory.
He calls me King David and says I should try
some of his stew. It will give me strength,
the strength he must have at night for the women.
We laugh loud like sultans and kings.

I would like to write a few lines
that could last a week like Sharif's stew,
that would fill the air of kitchens,
because I have no prayers
and no recipe for my faith—
a few lines that could
linger in my palms
and not be washed away.

Museum   **by Robert Hass**

On the morning of the Käthe Kollwitz exhibit, a young man and woman
come into the museum restaurant. She is carrying a baby; he carries the
air-freight edition of the Sunday *New York Times*. She sits in a high-
backed wicker chair, cradling the infant in her arms. He fills a tray with
fresh fruit, rolls, and coffee in white cups and brings it to the table. His
hair is tousled, her eyes are puffy. They look like they were thrown
down into sleep and then yanked out of it like divers coming up for air.
He holds the baby. She drinks coffee, scans the front page, butters a roll
and eats it in their little corner in the sun. After a while, she holds the
baby. He reads the *Book Review* and eats some fruit. Then he holds the
baby while she finds the section of the paper she wants and eats fruit and
smokes. They've hardly exchanged a look. Meanwhile, I have fallen in
love with this equitable arrangement, and with the baby who cooperates
by sleeping. All around them are faces Käthe Kollwitz carved in wood
of people with no talent or capacity for suffering who are suffering the
numbest kinds of pain: hunger, helpless terror. But his young couple is
reading the Sunday paper in the sun, the baby is sleeping, the green has
begun to emerge from the rind of the cantaloupe, and everything seems
possible.

Eve   **by Annie Finch**

When mother Eve took the first apple down
from the tree that grew where nature's heart had been
and came tumbling, circling, rosy, into sin,
which goddesses were lost, and which were found?
What spirals moved in pity and unwound
across our mother's body with the spin
of planets lost for us and all her kin?
What serpents curved their mouths into a frown,
but left their bodies twined in us like threads
that lead us back to her? Her presence warms,
and if I follow closely through the maze,
it is to where her remembered reaching spreads
in branching gifts, it is to her reaching arms
that I reach, as if for something near to praise.

The Clover   by W. S. Merwin

Well, I would say at last, when I had come in from that day's
mountain, I will go out now and mow a little patch of that clover, this
evening, for the beast. And I would take my scythe and sharpen it, with a
sound like the strokes of a dissolving bell. At that hour the heat would
have begun to leave the air. The shadows would have groped a long way
toward the ruined east. A coolness would be seeping through the stems
of the clover, near the ground at first, but beginning to rise. The moles
would have heard it. The mice would be running through it, small gray
teeth from no combs. And the leaves themselves would be starting to put
aside the gray mask they turn to the sun. They would be rising like green
skies, each stamped with one print of the same horse, each marked with a
single broken orbit, each mourning a short-lived star. The dew would
have just begun to come home to them from the sky, where it had been
hiding. Well, I would say after a while, I will go out and cut an armload
of that good clover for the beast.

The beast would watch me sharpening the scythe by the water
trough, in whose surface the first lamp was not yet lit. It would watch
me take down from the peg the folded square of old sacking for carrying
home the clover. I would look at the eyes of the beast and see that the
night was already there, and I would go out, with the folded sacking on
my shoulder and the gray blade glinting.

And there would be the clover, stretching before me, the nation
of shadow. I would go along the mossed wall to the stone gate and step
through into the field. And step into the secret breathing of the clover,
with my scythe. And there, the patch that I had thought to mow, the
same, the very patch that I had seen in the late day of my mind—some-
one would have mown it before me. Someone would have already mown
it. The same scythe-shaped segment, the same broken orbit, the same
silent smile. Someone else had come and made them. And taken that
clover. I would stand there in the little sudden breeze of twilight like a
third gate-post. And no one would come. No one would pass. No one
would tell me anything.

Evening after evening it would happen and at first I would cut
some other place—what I had thought of as some other evening's clover,
or I would take something else back for the beast. To no purpose. What
I put in the manger was never touched. I watched the beast carefully, the
deep fireless eyes, the nose like a rock out of a waterfall. Nothing
seemed wrong. The breath as sweet as ever, the movements as placid,

the coat as smooth. The udder as heavy, or heavier. I would pull up the three-legged stool and start milking. At the time I was living on little but that milk. And it was as sweet and rich and plentiful as ever. Who was feeding the beast? And better than I?

When I had drunk I would lean back in the straw, against the wall by the door, and watch my own thin blade set behind me, in the shadow. I would sit and watch the black clover growing in the sky. I would watch.

odes

Sunday Greens

by Rita Dove

She wants to hear
wine pouring.
She wants to taste
change. She wants
pride to roar through
the kitchen till it shines
like straw, she wants

lean to replace
tradition. Ham knocks
in the pot, nothing
but bones, each
with its bracelet
of flesh.

The house stinks
like a zoo in summer,
while upstairs
her man sleeps on.
Robe slung over
her arm and
the cradled hymnal,

she pauses, remembers
her mother in a slip
lost in blues,
and those collards,
wild-eared,
singing.

Ode on a Beet   by Vivian Shipley

> *All ye need to know*
> John Keats

Boil raw beets for the pleasure
of it, the old way of it, the work of it,
curly green leaves whistling
to bloody veins. Sunflowers race
for sky, untrellised peas languish,
but beets survive shade of cucumber
too nearly planted. Into yoga, beets

don't fight for space, or compete
with zucchini. Beet nubs heave,
grow, big or tiny, fissure at the neck.
Large beets peel naturally, small beets
are reluctant, not ripe. Greens steamed,
nubs boiled, cold garnet liquid saved
for dye, wanting this world to be
enough, I leave a taste of dirt, of earth.

First Radish   by Tamara Kaye Sellman

You pinch it gingerly
between finger and thumb
half an inch of red-white ball
a green ponytail sprouted
from its top, pale taproot
thin as a tendril of hair
quivering from the other end
of the globe

You sing it, over and over—
> *a little tiny baby*
> *a little tiny baby*
while I thin rapini in the garden,
give it grow-room for new roots,

harvesting these tenderlings
for tonight's April salad
    a little tiny baby
    a little tiny baby
Inside, as I rinse the hairy
root-legs of my thinnings,
I baptize your living marble
under cold streams of water,
pluck its sprightly crest,
leave the earnest three-week
root. You take it on your tongue
like a Host, and munch. My

fresh-scrubbed Cherry Belle,
you want to trust, to like
this thing you eat, but your face
betrays its bitter heat. When
I ask you if you like it, wide
brown eyes lie: *Yes.* I watch
you chew the morsel slowly,
cheeks flushed pink, determined.

Produce Aisle   by Rebecca McClanahan

The artichoke keeps her distance.
She has been taken too many times. Now
the armadillo armor hides her secret heart.

Everyone counts on the onion, staple of stews
and pottage. But deep in the crowded bin, her skin
is thin as moth wing. It peels away before their eyes.

Green peppers are modern women who take
their muscles seriously. They hunch their shoulders,
broad, shiny beneath a fluorescent sun.

Close by in cellophane the carrots keep for weeks,
the last to lose their figures. All legs,
tapering to slim ankles—and above,

wild profusion of hair. They gather in knots
of conversation and whisper about the apples,
those aging showgirls who didn't know when to quit,

redheads buffed an unnatural blush, a shine
that shouts *forever* while inside the white flesh softens.
In the center aisle, bananas in bunches

curl like firm young girls in sleep. Soon they will turn
like their half-price sisters, learn the bruise,
dark print that begins beneath the skin and grows.

Oh to be the avocado! She ages so well.
Time makes love to her daily, finding her sweeter
the softer she grows. Beside her the potato,

peasant woman in brown, comes into her own slowly.
She stays in the shadows, blindly remembers
her place. *Come to me! I will make you whole!*

coos the eggplant mother. And from the corner bin
a chorus: *Oranges, Oranges, Oranges, Oranges.*
We are what we seem. We speak our own name.

Grapefruit   by Gerald Stern

I'm eating breakfast even if it means standing
in front of the sink and tearing at the grapefruit,
even if I'm leaning over to keep the juices
away from my chest and stomach and even if a spider
is hanging from my ear and a wild flea
is crawling down my leg. My window is wavy
and dirty. There is a wavy tree outside
with pitiful leaves in front of the rusty fence
and there is a patch of useless rhubarb, the leaves
bent over, the stalks too large and bitter for eating,
and there is some lettuce and spinach too old for picking

beside the rhubarb. This is the way the saints
ate, only they dug for thistles, the feel
of thorns in the throat it was a blessing, my pity
it knows no bounds. There is a thin tomato plant
inside a rolled-up piece of wire, the worms
are already there, the birds are bored. In time
I'll stand beside the rolled-up fence with tears
of gratitude in my eyes. I'll hold a puny
pinched tomato in my open hand,
I'll hold it to my lips. Blessed art Thou,
King of tomatoes, King of grapefruit. The thistle
must have juices, there must be a trick. I hate
to say it but I'm thinking if there is a saint
in our time what will he be, and what will he eat?
I hated rhubarb, all that stringy sweetness—
a fake applesauce—I hated spinach,
always with egg and vinegar, I hated
oranges when they were quartered, that was the signal
for castor oil—aside from the peeled navel
I love the Florida cut in two. I bend
my head forward, my chin is in the air,
I hold my right hand off to the side, the pinkie
is waving; I am back again at the sink;
oh loneliness, I stand at the sink, my garden
is dry and blooming. I love my lettuce, I love
my cornflowers, the sun is doing it all,
the sun and a little dirt and a little water.
I lie on the ground out there, there is one yard
between the house and the tree; I am more calm there
looking back at this window, looking up
a little at the sky, a blue passageway
with smears of white—and grey—a bird crossing
from berm to berm, from ditch to ditch, another one,
a wild highway, a wild skyway, a flock
of little ones to make me feel gay, they fly
down the thruway, I move my eyes back and forth
to see them appear and disappear, I stretch
my neck, a kind of exercise. Ah sky,
my breakfast is over, my lunch is over, the wind
has stopped, it is the hour of deepest thought.
Now I brood, I grimace, how quickly the day goes,

how full it is of sunshine, and wind, how many
smells there are, how gorgeous is the distant
sound of dogs, and engines—Blessed art Thou,
Lord of the falling leaf, Lord of the rhubarb,
Lord of the roving cat, Lord of the cloud.
Blessed art Thou oh grapefruit King of the universe,
Blessed art Thou my sink, oh Blessed art Thou
Thou milkweed Queen of the sky, burster of seeds,
Who bringeth forth juice from the earth.

Recurring   **by Maggie Anderson**

The potatoes dream black smell of water deep
underground. They hold each other by ragged
strings and swish green headdresses in small
pools of mud. Potatoes dream their own
genetics, the predictable gossip of growth.
And they keep on dreaming it: the useless
berries their leaves invent, the digging out,
the clean uplifting, then the root cellar, one
slice saved to plant again in freezing ground.

Insomnia   **by Maggie Anderson**

The radishes pace in their red plaid bathrobes
and wish for sleep. They grow up and down
simultaneously and are preoccupied. Their green
tops keep them awake like fast conversation
they feel compelled to be in on, while
the white tangled threads of their pale roots
drag them down. They should have said something
else. They flush and fidget in the light topsoil
like reprimanded pups. Radishes sear the tongue,
the aftertaste of vigilance. They dream the burning
need for dream, the black dirt that won't go away,
the fear of intimacy, of breathing.

Black Olives   by Michael Waters

In those days while my then-wife
taught English to a mustached young nurse who hoped to join
her uncle's practice in Queens,
I'd sip gin on our balcony and listen to her
read aloud from the phrasebook,
then hear the student mimic, slowly, *Where does it hurt?*
then my wife repeat those words
so the woman might enunciate each syllable,
until I could no longer
bear it, so I'd prowl the Ambelokipi district
attempting to decipher
titles emblazoned on marquees—*My Life As A Dog,*
Runaway Train, Raging Bull—
then stroll past dark shops that still sold only one item—
kerosene, soap, cheese, notebooks—
to step down into the shop that sold olives, only
olives in barrels riddling
a labyrinth of dank aisles and buttressing brick walls.
I'd sidle among squat drums,
fingering the fruit, thumbing their inky shine, their rucked
skins like blistered fingertips,
their plump flesh, the rough salts needling them, judging their cowled
heft, biding my time. Always
I'd select a half-kilo of the most misshapen,
wrinkled and blackest olives
sprung from the sacred rubble below Mt. Athos, then
had to shout "Fuck Kissinger!"
three times before the proprietor would allow me
to make my purchase, then step
back out into the smut-stirred Athens night to begin
the slow stroll home, bearing now
my little sack of woe, oil seeping through brown paper,
each olive brought toward my mouth
mirroring lights flung from marquees and speeding taxis,
each olive burning its coal-
flame of bitterness and history into my tongue.

Finding Peaches in the Desert   by Pamela Uschuk

They taste like a woman, you say
and bite deep into the sweet heat
squeezing through tender skin,
while I laugh, taking the fruit you offer.
We close our eyes and transport
this delicious host to our loves
flown distant as time in dreams.
You can never eat too many, I say and pull
another ripe peach from the desert tree.
It fills my palm, my mouth as I suck
the unhusbanded nectar.
It is delicious as stealing light,
such innocent grace, a holiday
from history and eternity.
We bare our breasts to sun
as women have done for centuries
beside the blue water pool at ease with rabbits, shrill
wasps, the shy steps of occasional deer,
while vultures funnel midheaven.
Struck dumb by sun cauterizing
the Sonoran sky that flings its blue skirt
all the way across the ripe hip of Mexico,
we feast on peach after peach, while
peach-colored tanagers, wet
green hummingbirds and the topaz eyes of lizards
attend our annointment.
When I wipe one quarter across my breasts
and down my stomach to my thighs, I
am amazed at the baked odor of love
rising from everything I touch.
This is our ceremony to alter the news
of troops that mass for attack
in the Middle East, to alchemize all hatred
and greed, whatever name
it is given by multinational interests.
There is no aggression in sharing rare fruit
priceless as the wide imaginings of sky
or the brilliant coinage of dragonfly wings.

Even squadrons of wasps and fire ants
armed with nuclear stingers turn
from attack to the pungency of this
ritual feast that celebrates love
in the desert stunned green by unusual rain.

Avocado   **by John Logan**

> *for Robert Bly*

It is a green globe like a vegetable light bulb
with a stem to meet either soil or small living tree;
it is mottled like an old man's face or is wizened
like the enormous head of a fetus. Now the stem
has come away from a navel.
It has the stolid heft of a stone. The smell seeps up
and leads the mind far away to the earth's ancient cave.
Its taste is also pungent dirt with a kind of bark
that is quite difficult to chew:
here is the small tomb of woman.
Mother smells its fresh soil even with her dead sense. She feels
its husk. Her body inside is the soft flesh of fruit,
and her heart this oval green core.
Her grief, her anger is that she
no longer has life, but the stuff of her breathes a res-
idue that has remained in earth
and in the minds of the children.
Oh, now I know her skin sighs green

as this fluted fruit: her spirit
is the taste of it, transmuted.

> *Honolulu*
> *January 30, 1981*

Ode to a Lebanese Crock of Olives   by Diane Wakoski

for Walter's Aunt Libby's
diligence in making olives

As some women love jewels
and drape themselves with ropes of pearls, stud their ears
with diamonds, band themselves with heavy gold,
have emeralds on their fingers or
opals on white bosoms,
I live with the still life
of grapes whose skins frost over with the sugar forming inside,
hard apples, and delicate pears;
cheeses,
from the sharp fontina, to icy bleu,
the aromatic chevres, boursault, boursin, a litany of
thick bread, dark wines,
pasta with garlic,
soups full of potato and onion;
and butter and cream,
like the skins of beautiful women, are on my sideboard.

These words are to say thank you
to
Walter's Aunt Libby
for her wonderful olives;
oily green knobs in lemon
that I add to the feast when they get here from Lebanon
(where men are fighting, as her sisters have been fighting
for years, over whose house the company stays in)
and whose recipes for kibbee or dolmas or houmas
are passed along.

I often wonder,
had I been born beautiful,
a Venus on the California seashore,
if I'd have learned to eat and drink so well?
For, with hummingbirds outside my kitchen window to remind of small
elegance,
and mourning doves in the pines & cedar, speaking with grace,
and the beautiful bodies

of lean blond surfers,
dancing on terraces,
surely had I a beautiful face or elegant body,
surely I would not have found such pleasure
in food?
I often wonder why a poem to me
is so much more like a piece of bread and butter
than like a sapphire?
But with mockers flying in and out of orange groves,
and brown pelicans dipping into the Pacific,
looking at camelias and fuchsia,
an abundance of rose, and the brilliant purple ice plant
which lined the cliffs to the beach,
life was a "Still Life" for me.
And a feast.
I wish I'd known then
the paintings of Rubens or David,
where beauty was not only
thin, tan, California girls,
but included all abundance.

As some women love jewels,
I love the jewels of life.
And were you,
the man I love,
to cover me (naked) with diamonds,
I would accept them too.

Beauty is everywhere,
in contrasts and unities.
But to you, I could not offer the thin tan fashionable body
of a California beach girl.
Instead, I could give the richness of burgundy,
dark brown gravies,
gleaming onions,
the gold of lemons,
and some of Walter's Aunt Libby's wonderful olives from Lebanon.

Thank you, Aunt Libby,
from a failed beach girl,
out of the West.

1975

Cafeteria   **by Charlene Fix**

It's the long line I remember best,
and getting giddy in it with my friend Randy
while we waited for our meals
in that dormitory complex built for us
at the state college trying to absorb our numbers.
These days I get silly after eating,
drunk, as it were, on food, the assimilation of it
aging me beyond recall and the joke vast,
but then, the silliness came before.
Nineteen, in a press of nineteen-year-olds,
Randy and I would double-team a quiet guy
who worked in the cafeteria. We would flank him
and whisper God-knows-what in his ears, and laugh and laugh
though he would say nothing, our straight man,
but keep inching back with his broom for more
while the big Midwestern sun would invade the wall of windows,
dividing its rays among each, and shake into life the entire room
where we waited for the day to begin, and also
for white bread toast and powdered scrambled eggs
slapped up on plates on the counter.
And every morning we would tease that boy
whose name I'd resurrect if I could, whose name and face
I might even trade my own for, because I have to tell you
that in the midst of all that adolescent furor,
while there blazed far away a war we were safe from,
the boy we loved to tease, who was quiet and tall and lean with his broom,
went home for Christmas and skated on a pond.
When we returned three weeks later and looked for him,
Randy's curly hair bobbing, her full lips just wanting to laugh,
he was gone. We asked the woman in the shower cap,
where was the boy we had given a particularly rowdy sendoff to,
and she told us, in the slimness of time it took
to hand us our plates of steaming food.

love

The Woman Who Loved to Cook   by Erica Jong

Looking for love, she read cookbooks,
She read recipes for *tartelettes,*
terrines de boeuf, timbales,
& Ratatouille.
She read cheese fondue
& Croque Monsieur,
& Hash High Brownies
& Lo Mein.

If no man appeared who would love her
(her face moist with cooking,
her breasts full of apple juice
or wine),
she would whip one up:
of gingerbread,
with baking powder
to make him rise.

Even her poems
were recipes.
"Hunger," she would write, "hunger."
The magic word to make it go away.
But nothing filled her up
or stopped that thump.
Her stomach thought it was a heart.

Then one day she met a man,
his cheeks brown as gingerbread,
his tongue a slashed pink ham
upon a platter.
She wanted to eat him whole
& save his eyes.
Her friends predicted he'd eat her.

How does the story end?
    You know it well.

    She's getting fatter

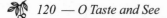

 & she drinks too much.
Her shrink has read her book
& heard her tale.

"Oral," he says,
& coughs
& puffs his pipe.

"Oral,
he says,
& now
"time's up."

Reading the Menu   **by Natasha Sajé**

*This is my favorite
part of the meal,*

she says, looking
up at her friend with eyes

bright as coins in water.
It's when the artichokes

are so young they can be
eaten raw; when the coriander-

rubbed tuna with tamari
vinaigrette is medium-

rare; when the Kiwano melon
lemon ice lasts; and when

the Barolo's bloom waits
to fill the air with berry

and leather.

At this moment
the past is a small mouse

twinkling around the edges
of the room, the future sits

like a pasha on his throne
and the present's diaphanous

peignoir of words
makes them forget

what hasn't been offered.

The Baking   by Larry Smith

A man and a woman are baking bread. They press their hands
into the dough and think of children.

In kitchen light the forms are danced into being, lifted into pans,
and sailed into the oven. The man and woman nod and caress each
other's hands. Their movement is a whisper.

While the oven is baking they lie naked on a bed. They bathe in
each other's touch. Their breathing is a song. Soon birds have gathered
outside their windows, waiting to be fed.

The man and the woman rise to feed the cries of birds and each
other, to open the doors of the oven and meet the children within.

Courting Game   by Judith Strasser

Is it true that you women set traps
for all of us skittery men? you ask
as you pour me a glass of champagne.

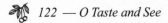

I imagine chubby Cupid, bare-bottomed

and bow in hand, but I'm not about to
commit. It was you who fed me pheasant
breast, warned me to watch for shot
just a moment before my filling edged

your hunter-brother's lead. I picture
your friend who ties his own flies,
carefully placing his line. *I'm more
of a worm-and-treble-hook guy,* you said.

In the snapshot you sent, you are trolling.
Once I caught rainbows myself: it was June,
ice still rimmed the cirque, the fish
were so hungry they weren't fair game.

Later, you quiver and twitch, the shaft
of an arrow that's fetched its mark
or a shimmering silver-backed trout
that has struck at my Mayfly lure.

Ever After   **by Joyce Stuphen**

What am I to you now that you are no
longer what you used to be to me?

Who are we to each other now that
there is no us, now that what we once

were is divided into me and you
who are not one but two separate and

unrelated persons except for that ex-
that goes in front of the words

that used to mean me, used to mean
you, words we rarely used (husband, wife)

as when we once posed (so young and helpless)
with our hands (yours, mine) clasped on the knife

that was sinking into the tall white cake.
All that sweetness, the layers of one thing

and then another, and then one thing again.

Cheese Log   by David Starkey

One week, I decide to buy a cheese log.
Unaccountably, my wife is appalled.
She begs me to buy beer, to buy beefy jerky,
to buy Bugles or Godzilla fruit snacks,
anything else. The cheese log is the color
of late pumpkins. Sharp cheddar sprinkled with
sliced almonds. We stand in the aisle arguing
until the prim store manager insists
that we pipe down. But I am implacable.
Finally, my wife admits that the cheese log
reminds her of a former lover, one
I never knew she had. It is like Gretta
and Michael Furey in James Joyce's "The Dead."
Old women stand weeping among the pork chops.
Snow is general throughout the frozen foods.

Bread and Sex at Midsummer   by Betty Greenway

      I look in book after book but find
            there's no such thing as a recipe, really.
Just keep that flour handy—
you might need a little more today,
or maybe not so much, if hoary-headed frost
should charm this summer into winter,
the furnace coughing phlegm so thick
that windows sweat, noses run,

or puckish cats lick butter from the bowl
so carefully set out to warm,
the honey dribble,
Madeira disappear.

Then yeast. Just sprinkle it on liquid
warm as blood that's breathing hard
and wait—

               froth on beer or cream on milk.

Now mix, until stiff enough to pull
from the bowl and knead—pressing,
turning, flipping, pressing,
lightly or roughly, just enough.

You'll know when it's ready.

Oil is called for here, to ease
the dough for its slow rise.

Sometimes more than once.

Don't hurry.

Finally, the oven preheated, you slip
it in and let it work.
Baking bread. Sex.

It's so obvious.

And after all that, sometimes
what you get you could live on
for years, aromatic, crust brown
hard and hollow,
inside, spun gold like fairies' wings
dancing naked in moonlight revels,
just like the picture, and sometimes,
no matter what or how hard
you wish upon a star, when you wake
you're an ass, or you've fallen
in love with one.

The Art of Love   by Karen Kovacik

I learned in my mother's kitchen, at her hands,
how to whip egg whites cleanly in a bowl,
till they billowed up like a ballerina's skirt,
then dropped like a curtsey on the pie.
I loved to scrape the skin from Jonathans
in curling strips and watch buds of chocolate
sweat saucily, dissolve to glossy waves,
while she supervised, gave orders, held me
to her standards. That's why I prefer it
alone now, no hand on the knife but mine,
my sole mistress of delight as I
melt and simmer my way to our repast.
Such priestly offices, chaste discipline!
Sweetheart, I don't want you to watch. You're not
of this order. I, too, have hung around
kitchens of former loves, watching Frank
chop cilantro and chiles, Michael shape
croissants. Like you, I too tried to steal sips,
beg hugs, slip my hand under a belt, but
preoccupied, they bristled with reproof.
Just *wait*. After I steam the rice, reduce
the sauce, sauté the chicken with tarragon
and grapes, after I watch every morsel
disappear, then, satisfied that you are
satisfied, I'll let you lay hands on me.

Desire   by Kathy Fagan

How the melody of a single ice cream truck
can rise from the streets of your city
and bring with it every year you have ever known.
How it can bring forth children
and the promise that has always belonged to them
and the shining dimes and the rush of icy vapors
from the truck's freezer to the sky.
How it rises past the green froth of maple leaves

to your windows as if to say, *Summer already*,
here for you and haven't they always been?
And haven't you given each one of them away,
your arms lifted, your mouth opened
for the cool winds of October?
Yes, you think, on the other side of the country
in the long tanned valleys of California,
the fiddle-neck curls upon itself and crows pull
every living morsel from the soft ground.
And farther west, on the warming coastal rocks
of the Pacific, crabs raise their one good arm
to the sun—like the farmer in China you imagine
or the dusty pistils of tulips in Europe. But you
have to be here, listening to an incessant song and children
who want, who want, no more and no less than yourself.
Tell your sorrow to the gulls that flail outside
your window, too far inland for their own good.
they could be at any shore but they are here
and isn't that all they're good for:
to be screamed at, to scream back?
Tell it to the man who shares your bed
and he will weight his head more deeply
into his pillow, touching your hand out of habit,
taking you ever farther from the life you wanted
as if you ever wanted a life, as if your many mounting desires
led to no more than the final consolation of silence
and the long dreamless sleep of those who hunger for nothing.
That is the lie we tell ourselves—that we can do without
this life. For if night darkened our eyes and our very hearts
turned cold as the moon, then wouldn't you
take it all back if you could? Three thin dimes in your pocket
and the music of a truck close to your ear and the summer
already moist in your armpits—don't you want to wrap your lips
around the melting sweetness of it? Won't you pay
and keep paying for as long as you must, to know
it belongs, has always belonged, to you?

End Pieces   **by Paola Corso**

She sat her husband down
made the confession she stole food
from the refrigerator

You mean our refrigerator? You didn't steal nothin'.

Lou, I ate a sweet pickle and two slices of bread.
The end pieces.

That food's yours, Flo! I bought that for you to eat.

I didn't ask first.

You don't have to for Chris'sake. This is your home.

She opened the refrigerator
made herself an egg and fried Jumbo
He went next door to tell his sister

What does she know anymore, Lou.

She usedta grow her own cucumbers and can 'em.
Put Heinz to shame. And baked every week, too.
Bread and somethin' sweet.

Forget about it. What's said is said.

Worked half her life at Liberty Mirror.
Brought home a steady paycheck and this is
what it comes down to. Over a goddam pickle
and two heels she hasta ask first!

Fran just told me there's going to be more layoffs.
The lucky ones who keep their jobs have to take pay cuts.
Do you think the big cheeses bothered to ask first?
For something like that!?
That's more than a couple of heels out of the fridge.

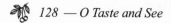

He waved his hand in disgust
left for the Giant Eagle
bought groceries for him and Flo

She was alone with four slices of bread
two sweet pickles, floating
in a jar of green juice and seeds

Mussels   by Ingrid Wendt
For Ralph

We've learned where the big ones grow,
to harvest not from the tops of rocks where shells
fill with sand

to follow the tide out to the farthest reefs we can reach
and still not get wet, where last time we found
giant anemones green-sheathed and dripping under

the overhangs like the cocks of horses, we laughed, or
elephants, having each come to the same conclusion,
fresh from bed and married long enough

to say such things to each other, again
to remember the summer we first discovered mussels
big as fists protecting Sisters Rocks.

Just married and ready for anything, even
mussels were game, black as obsidian, stubbornly
clinging to rocks, to each other, their shells

so tightly together we had to force them apart
with a knife, the meat
inside a leap of orange, poppy-bright; and when

three perch in a row took the hook you'd baited
tender as liver we said we must try them ourselves
someday, if they're safe, which they weren't

all the years we lived down south: red algae in summer
tides infiltrating our chance to experiment, food without precedent,
how would we know what to do?

Counting at last on friends who had been to Europe and now
are divorced, we waded waist deep to pick some,
scraping our knuckles raw on barnacles

none of us knowing to soak our catch two hours at least
to clean out the sand; the sand we took in with butter and lemon
cleaning our teeth for a week.

Now we can't get our fill of them.
Weekend vacations you work to the last, cooking
one more batch to freeze for fritters or stew.

Now we harvest them easily, take the right tools, wear boots
we gave to each other for birthdays so we don't have
to remember to watch out for waves

to feel barnacles unavoidably crushed underfoot
like graveyards of dentures waves have exposed, although
sometimes now I find myself

passing over the biggest, maybe because
they've already survived the reach of starfish,
blindly prowling on thousands of white-tipped canes,

or they've grown extra barnacles,
limpets, snails, baby anemones,
rock crabs hiding behind. As though

age after all counts for something
and I've grown more tender-hearted,
wanting you not to know about the cluster

I found today, for the first
time in years having taken time off from job
and housework and child care, sleeping so late

my feet got wet on the incoming tide, unexpectedly
talking aloud, saying look at that one, bigger even
than Sisters Rocks: a kind of language

marriage encourages, private as memories of mussels,
anachronistic as finding I miss you
picking mussels to take home to you

not the ones you'd pick if you could but fresh
as any young lover's bouquet and far more edible,
more than enough to last us at least a week.

Eating Soba   **by David Hassler**

I speak your language when I eat—
the silence of steam and scent
rising to me; red pepper, ginger, and soy.
This bowl's heat in my hands.
I snap apart chopsticks,
break the yoke of the raw egg
they call Full Moon that drifts
in the center as though in a pond.
I pull the soba noodles to my mouth
and hiss, un-making their long strings.
This is the sound of eating soba,
sucking in air, loud and energetic.
I hear wood rasp and tap
inside the bowls as they are drained
and clacked down on the counter empty.
Customers come and go through
the heat and steam of these small
kitchen shops, ordering soba,
soba o-kudasai!
I bow over your bowl
your body, your broth.
These are my hands that hold you.
This is the sound of my lips, warm
breathing you in
saying soba!

Song of Separation 2   **by Stuart Lishan**

Sunday morning in the market:
A bright display of cherries and pears,
          like a dozen peacocks sleeping.
               These little generosities of love.

Just off the brick path
          hidden near the lilac bush,
          a transcendence of tiger lilies.

The chop chop chop of a knife—
          basil, freshly picked from the garden:
          A husband making dinner for his wife.
                         *

Such is the crazy babble of August nights:
          The creaking of an empty house:
     Bosnia's tribal violence
                    humming from the TV,
                              as he eats the meal
               when his wife doesn't come home;

                         *

     the ratchets, the whines of bugs,
          his mind like a raven rasping
          unsoftened by summer winds;

                         but not once her step, not once
          her voice stepping home
          through the loud screen door.

What I Thought I Was Eating by Jared Carter

was what they set in front of me on long strips of paper
        torn from a roll and spread out over the tables: food
brought by the people who worshipped there, each according
        to his or her time in the congregation. Casseroles
and green beans and potatoes brought by the Young Marrieds,
        the chicken fried by the Men's Class, the salad provided
by the choir, the soft drinks iced down and kept in a big tank
        floating with blocks of ice by the Philathea Co-Workers,
the banana cream pie and chocolate bundt cake by the Senior
        Women, coffee brewed in a ceramic urn by the Senior Men
who handed it to me in a paper cup when I walked in and knew
        whether I took cream or sugar, and called me
by my first name. The flowers on the tables arranged
        by the preacher's wife. The time when the preacher
himself spread out his arms, and in a strong voice asked
        everyone for silence, and began to say grace. That
was what they offered me, what I was taking, no
        questions asked, and glad to have. It was enough, too.

Partytime, Joanna— by Bonnie Jacobson

Time to curry the eggs and mull the wine.
Set up the cellist and stir the spouse.
Fluff the children and fling open the door to
all those who have flung open theirs, beaming
welcome to our privacy, slip from your wrap
yes I can see yours is an enviable blouse
so lovely this occasional intimacy
have you met let us pour we're just back.
Time to gather at the window, note
another sun is dying *always so sad* when
its red eye sinks *titanic but what can*
you do night is a bitch and promiscuous
—or so the olive gossips on the stem,
so the hour murmurs, so the eyes move in the room—

Oh where is it *the time of our lives*?
Quick, Joanna, light another candle,
light a crystal chandelier, a crackling fire,
a pêche flambé. Insist they *cannot go*
and embrace them as they go. Wave, wave to
the lingerers handed into their cars, wave
to their slim parade through the gate.
Then walk the dog slowly. Pause.
The Dipper is stars pouring stars.
They are more beautiful than they know.
And the last crystal fragments of snow.
And the dog, ready now to curl and sleep.

After the Muffin   by Robert Brimm

You've something on
your lip, you say,
your finger, gentle
as a kiss, floating
to show me where.

Blueberry! For
we have just shared
a warm muffin
by candlelight.

And now, all these
hours later, I still
feel that touch
like a kiss, still
hear you saying:

You've something
on your lip.

My New Boyfriend   by Tara Miller

My new boyfriend sleeps in the refrigerator
sucks on lettuce leaves
writes poems on the out-
sides of jars with his finger
forgets my name when the light
blinks out.
Packages of sandwich meat accumulate
have the shape of a pillow
placed under hips
his long legs rest on plastic
cups of yogurt.
I hear him humming
when the refrigerator is silent
can almost recognize his meaning.
I suspect he has someone
sitting there beside him
some memory of some girl
so real
she too collects moisture on all sides.
This would explain the cleared second shelf
the poems.
He rarely comes out when I'm home
but I know
when I'm at work
he breathes the air in my house.
Footprints pace damp circles in the kitchen
climb the stairs
he sniffs the garments
tried on but not worn
in my lingerie drawer
drags
the scent back to the refrigerator.
My neighbors don't believe he's real.
But I know.
At night when he thinks I'm asleep
chilled hands roam my body
enter me

stay in my head, my dreams.
I forgive his need to burrow
to disappear when I need him
forgive the limited space
he allows
for other necessities.

My Last Two Wives

Ira Sadoff

My last two wives loved everything
about potatoes their ugly color their hopeless
shape they even loved the joke about potatoes
"What has a thousand eyes but cannot see?"
they loved to mash them
fry them boil them until they cried out for help
they loved to cut them open
just to see the cold cup of starch
lying still in its skin like a snowdrift

they could not live without potatoes
it was amazing like a bad habit
they could not stop
from grabbing potatoes off the counters
hiding them in their pocketbooks
and dreaming of endless tables of potatoes
weeping out of all their eyes
caressing them into sleeplessness
making them eat their own dirt

it is a wonder I could not love them

Sunday Morning   by Robert Fox

Her arm with the lymphedema bandage
flags me as I slip off the bed.
I lean close with my good ear.
She is awake now, too, though she went to bed much later.
Five hours of sleep is all Decadron will allow.
She offers to make breakfast for both of us,
something she has not done in longer
than I can remember. I fear disaster,
nothing will be done on time,
another meal mostly cold.
We agree on eggs and sausage patties.
I prepare my coffee and she is downstairs
faster than I expected. Before I know it
pans appear on the stovetop.
She reaches into the refrigerator,
the egg box slips from her hand
and the box lands upside down. Only one egg
cracked and will be scrambled.
I set the table, prepare toast,
watch her recent, unnatural heaviness
shuffle with difficulty
from the counter to the refrigerator.
I list what I have done so far
so that we are clear,
and stay out of her way,
except to check the eggs.
My feet tangle in the throwrug
by the table, a frequent source of contention.
I say nothing. I don't see the sausage.
Often she forgets.
I hadn't seen her slip the patties
into the oven on a cookie tin.
I peer at the eggs across the room
and start the toast.
Somehow, too, her tea is ready
on time. I don't know how
she has done this.

We sit together for breakfast
in an unrushed calm, reminiscent
of making love upon awaking
in the years before children.
Now we compare our sparse hair.
I tell her about the conference I just attended,
and we discuss how one identifies talent in the arts,
drift to the forthcoming presidential election.
We eat with the back door open.
Outdoors it is humid but cool.
The Rose of Sharon by the tree stump
blooms again in September
like all the years we've had together.

Da Capo   **by Jane Hirshfield**

Take the used-up heart like a pebble
and throw it far out.

Soon there is nothing left.
Soon the last ripple exhausts itself
in the weeds.

Returning home, slice carrots, onions, celery.
Glaze them in oil before adding
the lentils, water, and herbs.

Then the roasted chestnuts, a little pepper, the salt.
Finish with goat cheese and parsley. Eat.
You may do this, I tell you, it is permitted.
Begin again the story of your life.

Litany   **by Billy Collins**

> *You are the bread and the knife,*
> *The crystal goblet and the wine.*
>   Jacques Crickillon

You are the bread and the knife,
the crystal goblet and the wine.
You are the dew on the morning grass,
and the burning wheel of the sun.
You are the white apron of the baker
and the marsh birds suddenly in flight.

However, you are not the wind in the orchard,
the plums on the counter,
or the house of cards.
And you are certainly not the pine-scented air.
There is no way you are the pine-scented air.

It is possible that you are the fish under the bridge,
maybe even the pigeon on the general's head,
but you are not even close
to being the field of cornflowers at dusk.

And a quick look in the mirror will show
that you are neither the boots in the corner
nor the boat asleep in its boathouse.

It might interest you to know,
speaking of the plentiful imagery of the world,
that I am the sound of rain on the roof.

I also happen to be the shooting star,
the evening paper blowing down an alley,
and the basket of chestnuts on the kitchen table.

I am also the moon in the trees
and the blind woman's teacup.
But don't worry, I am not the bread and the knife.
You are still the bread and the knife.
You will always be the bread and the knife,
not to mention the crystal goblet and—somehow—
        the wine.

market

Spring

by Jane Galin

You hurt now, your lips and your hands
dipped in April's stinging melt—
old water
frozen over dust and leaf dust.
Another sun: rot begins again,
the throb, the flow and the ferment,
burning ice across our tilting planet.
Root throb;
winds confess in disappearing ink
their pasts of pollen, wings, salt and violence;
the sky darkens
and the dragged clouds spit.
An old tradesman sits in his clutter of wooden crates;
he splits a watermelon,
outs a red gust gasped into the wind—
You stop:
you see our lives' four seasons
in that swollen fruit, a world
as fast gone ripe
as summer sweetening in its green hug,
while the inevitable black seedfall,
the hard barter for our lusts,
interrupts the flesh
among the small white seeds,
impossible,
glimpsed, riddling,
refuse of the future snowing inside the heart.
The old man scolds and laughs; he knows
everyone is drunk with the new fruit-scented struggling winds,
the whirling dust, the voices,
and the plenty of oranges and plums.
His sweethearts gather around him, answering him
the way they always do,
the way they must in such a city
where torn love strews the streets,
everywhere, unable to perish,
like large fruit cumbrous on a delicate vine,
smashed, rotting among its own intact seeds.

from *Pike Market Variations*   **by Christopher Merrill**

O savor of salt
                    and salmon — the holy
And nomadic chinook
                    neatly filleted in ice;
The king and coho
                    caught by a troller
Or gleaned from a gill net,
                         gulls circling overhead;
And loaves of baked bread
                         steaming in waxed bags,
Salt-rising and sourdough,
                    the settlers' legacy;
And green onions, garlic,
                    goulash, and gazpacho;
And sweet-and-sour pork
                    simmering in the pot
Of the Chinese cook;
                    and chutney; and chocolate;
And lemons and loquats;
                    and loganberry jam;
— All gathered up and garnished
                         in gusts of salt air!

The fishmonger, fattened
                    on fried clams
And beer batter,
                    brandishes his knife
At the cat on the counter.
                         A woman in culottes
Buys ferns and freesias
                    at the flower shop,
Then roams around
                    the crowded block, reading
Menus, a mark
                    for the moneyed and the saved.
A futures trader tickles her
                         until she turns away.
A Moonie hails her,
                    and she hurries home

To sear and sauté
        for someone new.
O nights of white wine
        and high winds!
O curry, and cayenne,
        and sweetened cappuccino!

The Good House (Searching for Ragersville)   by Terry Hermsen

Blue eye above the earth
rides east with us. No rush, we
have the whole day.

Steam lifts from a farm pond
like a wide white tree
stretching its roots in the water.

Deeper in the hills, buggies spot
the towns: Berlin, Charm, Mt. Hope,
each with its Narrow Lane.

At the egg auction, wide with bleachers,
cartons mounded with brown shells, ours
are the only uncovered heads.

Gravel crossroads. Willow roots
above the draped stream.
We ask directions at the metal shop.

The father strokes his wire beard.
Outside, the youngest daughter plows the air
on her horseheaded swing.

On a slope above the edge of town
the good neighbors lie.
Yoder, Bessom, Gretzenmueller.

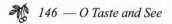

Ragersville: The Good House
stands like a yellow ghost
right up against the road.

Hair tied back, ex-biker, the cook
sits down with us, his legs bowed
around the chair, the wide room empty.

Laughing, he brings us all we can afford:
thick slabs of spiced portabello
with a side of edible flowers.

Breakfast at the County Seat Café   **by Jeff Gundy**

Someone turned the house into two dining rooms with the
kitchen between, this smallish one crammed with the end
of the morning rush, construction guys fueling their achy
get-it-done bodies, older men in no special hurry, wait-
resses bustling among us all. The only space is at the
counter right next to the register, last place I'd choose—I
always want my back to a wall.

But the grandmotherly waitress talks to me, brings more
bad coffee than I want, and I tune in to the hum and buzz
and feel all right. The eggs are big and cooked just so
and I eat the first piece of toast with them and the
second with the blackberry jam.

The guys stroll up to pay their $3.94 or 68 cents for just
coffee and maybe they notice me and maybe not but it's
safe as churches, I know I can say no thanks next time
the coffee comes around, I can pay and get out the door
before my stomach muscles clench entirely with caffeine
and the familiar strangeness of life a hundred miles from
home at the County Seat Café.

When the rush slacks off the waitresses wash and dry,
talk about another woman, the mall, some story. "She

thinks I'm telling stories? She knows more about me
than I know about her!" "That's right!" "I don't know
anything about her!" That's right.

I love the hidden hollows inside rooms, inside language. I
love to sit like a rock in the stream and wonder at the
burbling around me. I love the exclamation mark, the
dash, the waitresses bumping hips as they crowd past
each other with plates of eggs and sausage. I love that
half-laugh, the worlds inside it, the coins swept off the
counter and the near-clean rag behind, yellow gloves and
bruises at the hip and thigh, one more morning of men
who need food and coffee and talk and are willing and
able to pay.

For My Friends, Who Complain　　　　　**by William Greenway**
That I Never Write Anything Happy

>   I should go with him in the gloom,
>   Hoping it might be so.
> 　　　　　　　-"The Oxen," Thomas Hardy

Once when I was building a church
out in the country, Christmas coming,
shingles glittering like tinsel, bare trees
still flocked with frost, we broke for lunch,
the other wood butchers and me,
and went looking, found a nothing little
roadhouse, and not expecting anything
since things smell better outside than in,
we sat and ordered the special—meatloaf,
sweet potatoes, turnip greens, and corn bread.
It was so good we almost couldn't climb
the ladder, sang carols like drunks all afternoon,
beating time with our hammers on nails.
I've never had anything like it before
or since.
 Later the church burned down,
and I never could find that roadhouse again.

I've even lost the people who could prove
it happened at all, and though
it probably wouldn't be the same,
every Christmas I go home
and drive the back roads,
following no map
but my nose.

Elementary   by William Greenway

Monday they'd bring a quarter—I'd carry
another bag, creased and wet
from my fist, or box that was a tin
cartoon of leftovers. Down a long
row I walked for milk, past steel
pans steaming real food. Anything
gets old, perfect meatloaf, vine ripe
tomatoes—under desks they
harden, soften, exchange chemicals.
Some days I'd dump it all, even sandwiches
my blond mother made in darkness,
unopened into drums of pig slop and beg
hard rolls like Luke Butler,
who stank, had green clothes, free hot
lunches, and blackheads, volcanoes pricked
with pepper. I still get sick of what
I make myself, and crave, not Antoine's
or Maxim's, but the dawn bacon of summer
camps, mess halls, the cafeterias of prisons,
mental institutions, homes for the old.
And what is heaven but another leftover?
Although I hope it's a sort of higher school,
one you walk to with both hands open.

Highway 18, Fairfax, OK

by Nan Arbuckle

Saturday dinner at the Roller Inn—
chicken fry and refills on iced tea.
Cream gravy lapped thick
to the edges of the platter,
coated the brown steak, then
slid between fat french fries.
The meat soft and juicy,
fresh fried and stacked
like two light brown pancakes,
cut tender as toothless dreams.
Some people just don't know
how good greasy tastes.
One good mouthful and I was safe.
Quiet, calm. Home—right there
with deer heads and twenty-inch
rock bass. Home in a diner with not
a single picture of a walking horse
and no trace of tennessee accents,
Home, eight hundred miles and fifteen
years from Sundays at the Southland Cafe.

Midwest Albas

by Collette Inez

In heartland cafeterias, I hear
the resolute chirp of women
heaping pale food on white platters,
tuna surprise, baby corn niblets,
flash-frozen cod, potatoes
whipped, ridged, stuffed, mashed,
washed down with peach cobblers,
coconut pie, sighing under vanilla
ice cream in a scoop,
and loaves, wafers, snaps, strips,
squares, puffs, crullers, cakes,

guests at the wedding of lemon
and meringue, at the marriage of brown
and serve, humming in the company of veal,
sole in foil baked by midwestern women
offering consolations of buttermilk
biscuits, the solace of fritters,
throughout the breadbasket states of the land,
rendered helpless in a rain of salt,
in a meltdown of cream.

Table for One   by Francis J. Smith

I am a sucker for ambience.
Like the intimate French restaurant
downstairs, dim, with posters of Nice,
but "table for one" is awkward to say.
The waiter, proud of his massive menu,
led me to a niche in the corner
as if I were improperly dressed.

Then the whole bit—mussels meunière,
Dover sole with Montrachet in bucket,
chocolate mousse, coffee, and brie.
A petty hedonist out on a spree.

Mostly tables of double couples
smiling in starch and fur.
Time to muse, to stare
at honey-crusted bread, time
to play a role or wiggle toes.

Now, I am no fool for happiness.
I noted the lout who snapped at his love
till she left, looped, for the john
while he ogled the sultry one by the door,
but dining out alone is a bore.

FOUND POEM: How to Eat Lobster   **by Frank Polite**

Boiled:
First,
TWIST OFF THE CLAWS

CRACK
EACH CLAW
WITH A NUTCRACKER
or hammer
or anything handy

BREAK THE FLIPPERS OFF
the tailpiece

next
USE A FORK to push
the meat out of
the body

UNHINGE THE BACK
the " tomalley"
or liver, a delicacy
to many lobster
eaters, turns green
when boiled

OPEN THE BODY
Crack it sideways

THE SMALL CLAWS
are delicious eating
suck the meat out

Broiled:
TWIST OFF
the claws

THERE IS THIS DIFFERENCE
use the fork to lift
the meat

BREAK OFF SMALL CLAWS
suck meat out

PS
don't miss the " tomalley."

(place mat,
 GRANADA Restaurant,
Toledo, Ohio)

Hamburger Heaven   by Patti Capel Swartz

At twelve, I loved the Town Talk Diner
where greasy burgers, fries, and cherry cokes were the rage.
I went there every chance I had, even though Mother forbade me.
"Those boys there are up to no good," she admonished.
"Pool-hall hustlers, every mother's son of them."
Fascinated by one she held in least esteem
—shiny black hair slicked to a perfect D.A.,
turned up collar, leather Duke's jacket—
I slipped through the diner door, hoping he would look my way.
I thought him perfect.
Over the half-moon
of my half-eaten hamburger,
I watched with hungry eyes.

Two doors down was Aldom's Diner,
stainless steel trolley car converted to restaurant,
with counter, swiveling stools, and imitation leather booths.
Mother approved. It had, she said, a "family atmosphere."
"Nothing like that dingy dark hole where pool sharks hang out."
After basketball games on Saturday nights
my brother drove my junior-high friends and me there,
away from the sin, juicy as the grease that dripped down my chin,
of the Town Talk,
away from the heavenly grease on plate—and hair.

Several for the Road   by Cyril Dostal

Popcorn Poem
Eating popcorn on the interstate through the Poconos,
I throw some out the window to feed a bird I'll never see.

Chocolate-Covered Cherry Poem
Eating chocolate-covered cherries on the Ohio Turnpike,
I get one the cherry machine missed.

Ham Sandwich Poem
Eating a ham sandwich driving through the Adirondacks,
I want to holler out the window, *"Anyone for Mah-jong?"*

Black Coffee Poem
Drinking black coffee on the Indiana Toll Road.
I peer through misted tunnels of the night.

Fried Chicken Poem
Eating fried chicken on the Pennsylvania Turnpike,
I wipe my greasy fingers on my pants.

Pepsi-Cola Poem
Drinking warm Pepsi on the highway through Wisconsin,
I raise my can and toast the health of every passing herd.

Circus Peanuts Poem
Eating circus peanuts on the Tollway around Chicago,
I contribute empty shells in every basket with my change.

Dairy Queen Poem
Eating a Dairy Queen on State Route 2 in West Virginia,
I hold it out the window to let the drips fall off.

Washington State Apples Poem
Eating Washington State Apples on the New York Thruway,
I chuck my cores to do my share for reforestation.

Hard-Boiled Eggs Poem
Eating hard-boiled eggs on the New Jersey Turnpike,
I pray like hell for rain.

Sweet Red Peppers, Sun Drieds,   **by Martha Silano**
the Hearts of Artichokes

Pagliacci Pizza wants me.
Lying in bed on a Sunday morning,

I could almost want them back.

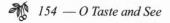

The trick, a deliverer said,

is learning to hesitate. Not in the car
or walking to the door, but just

inside, when they're waiting
for change.

Or I could manage a bingo hall,
swirl behind glass at the Lusty Lady.

Once it was a cornfield,
sixteen hours a day in a moving cage, reaching

for tassels. I've picked cherries, scooped
pickles, sold knives and rakes and

rolls that fell to the floor
while my bosses took up flying.

Maybe Pagliacci's wouldn't be bad.
Evenings. A car. The minor streets

of Queen Anne. And at the end
of my shift, I could settle in—eating
what got sent back.

To Market, to Market   **by Colleen McElroy**

on the levee the smell of smoked
fish separated me from my ill-earned
allowance quicker than the chepa ropes of red
licorice and packets of tart Koolaid
my St. Louis cousins constantly craved—
under the glass-domed market, everything imitated
what someone else had dreamed and square-tucked
into paper cartons, pure white as city fathers planned
but I was black and Catholic and needed a life made

possible by the brine of open seas and mysteries of finned
sunstreaks dancing on green oceans, a world I feared
and loved, fascinated as my grandma hummed
songs of Jesus' wealth while she beheaded
catfish or filleted carp already scaled—
at ten I almost knew how fish could hold a deep-seated
sense of magic despite man's prehistoric dread
of salty graves and red tides, so I traded
with gill-faced fishmongers who snickered and palmed
50¢ for half-spoons of fish eggs or lox glued
too thin to sheets of waxed paper, and later bus-bound
for home, my crimp-haired cousins wrinkled
their fat black noses and refused
to sit near me— "You were weirded
out," my daughter announces now when I feed
her tales of how even then I had a strange need
for the smelly magic of the sea, its fruit and tides—
water singing of countries yet to be tasted

Work, Thank, Eat   **by Daryl Ngee Chinn**

1. Second Cook

Work around
the cook and his temper.
When he wants radishes, Chinese parsley,
or green onions for garnishes,
have them washed and trimmed already.
When he wants to cook chicken,
he should find it plucked and cleaned.
When he chops cooked duck,
a serving plate should appear.
If he has to stir fry,
you deep fry.
If he needs to make a sauce,
put seasoning and cornstarch nearby.
After he dishes food, garnish it

and wash the pan.
If he rushes by or turns abruptly,
move aside like air.
If you are idle, wash dishes,
do something with the big knife,
whatever needs doing first.

2. Prayer

Variety,
black mushrooms, straw mushrooms,
bird's nest, crispy gai lon and bok choy,
hairy seaweed, shark fin, sea slug,
steamed pork with salt fish and ginger,
winter or hairy melon soup,
bitter melon with black beans,
cooked eggs cut like noodles,
radishes pared into birds and flowers,
calf brain soup, braised pig guts,
oxtail soup, white cut chicken,
tofu's sweet taste—

all this comes to you
from scarce wood,
scarce land,
many starved mouths.

3.

Please taste
some of everything.

Crab Festival in Henderson, Louisiana   **by Elton Glaser**
for Karen

Sweat and rain and the spiced waters
Running down a crab's dead leg—

All morning my sister and I

Kept up with the sun, a junket past Baton Rouge
And over the swills of the Mississippi, the car
Floating on a long bridge through swamps,
Then down a levee road, damp dirt and gravel,
Both of us out for more than
Blue bodies boiled to scarlet, more than a
Mouthful of yellow fat, or the sweet white wads inside;

Jaycees and ladies from the church
Roped up the banners, and opened the stands at noon,
Bowls of etouffée and okra gumbo, bottlenecks of beer
Breaking the ice in a washtub, and sno-cones
For the kids, a rainbow drip of syrup
Cool and sticky in the heat;

From the picnic pavilion, over a cheap PA,
The keen and fracas of a Cajun fiddle
Pulled us in, my sister sizzling in a two-step,
Fast feet on the concrete floor, before the old folks
Eased out, belly to belly in a bayou waltz,

While I watched, and drained a Dixie, and waited for
That flatbed parked at the end of the pleasure grounds
To rig its traps and mikes, dark faces of a bar band
Pale in the day's deep glare, and then the bass
And drums rumbling from the raw bottom of some R&B,
Smoky sway of a sax that strokes the appetite—

And now this late drizzle under the pines,
Tables sheeted with last week's news, and napkins
Ripped from a roll, where we pay to
Pound a knife handle against hard claws,
And split the cracked mosaic of the lower plates,
And scrape the dead man's chest out with the guts,
Our lips aching with cayenne, spitting back
The bay leaves and the black buckshot of coriander,
Hands wounded by shrapnel on the wet planks,

And all around us, elbow to shoulder, bench after bench,
The homely hierarchies of the South, from rednecks
With a jaw full of Red Man, to the ginghams of gossip,
Seersucker suits from the courthouse seated next to
T-shirts blazoned with heavy metal and the bible camps,
A feast of people busy in the rain, no melting pot,
But a cauldron of crabs baptized in hell, bubbling
And banging under furious water, a rough rite
That savors every lick and sip, even in this mud,
This air still seething with a sultry tang.

Understudy   by Daniel Lusk

Old men who eat alone in small cafes
arrange the silver carefully
beside the plate.

It crawls inside their cuffs
and edges out again along their temples
and the gothic arches of their brows.

Arranging is the life
now
isn't it.

Old men check their watches
frequently,
lest the sand run out unnoticed
onto the table by the water glass.

Their hands flutter
over the fork and spoon again, the knife,
as if the knife were a lost opportunity
or a love that might be set to rights.

Attentive as they are to these
small handles,

I suspect if they let go

they'll belly up with loneliness
and float off toward the ceiling fans
in all these small cafes

where I sit watching, hours on end,
to learn their little order,
eating alone.

Eating at Casa Blanca   **by Willis Barnstone**

Eating at Casa Blanca with my pen
  and paper, first I dip

warm bread in olive oil. Here I can
  scribble for an hour

all alone and eat crêpe manicotti
  spinach and drink the flower

of English Breakfast tea. The universe
  is intimate. We're friends.

She drops delicious in this verse.

world

Selections from *Asian Figures*   **translated by W. S. Merwin**

Bean seed
bean babies

*

Can't grow it
once you roast it

*

All right you've got nothing to
    give me
don't break my bowl

*

Too hot
no taste

*

Cow in the stream
eating from both banks

*

Even honey
tastes like medicine
when it's medicine

*

Everybody thinks
you had supper
at the other place

*

Nobody notices hunger
but nobody misses dirt

*

Coconut
has the moon inside
    *

Squash plant
child sits waiting
mother goes on climbing

*

If two men feed a horse
it will stay thin

*

Melon on a housetop
has two choices

Saigon Market Peace Talks Sutra   by Richard Hague

Over-The Rhine, Cincinnati, Ohio, 1998

Under a clear November sky,
three decades after Da Nang, My Lai,
after the Tet offensive, after the screaming
and blood on the letters home,
after the ghosts of boys stalking
canebrakes and glinting paddies,
this morning the Metro buses idle
fresh in their blues and whites, waiting
at the crosswalks, advertising hair rinse
and Volvos, while all the colors of things
here in the market—lemons, mangos, glinting bottles
on the curbs where winos drink—
shine twice or three times bright.

And I walk down Elder Street

toward Findlay Market's open-air fruit stalls and storefronts,
dudes hooting and hanging in the 'hood, eyeing
the girls who are with us on our writing and eating trip,
Carla, Melissa, Kathy, Meghan, not far from the smokes
of Mr. Pig's Ribs roasting in sidewalk barbecues
the size of small cars, not far from the steeples
of a dozen churches, old St. Mary's
with its Masses in cold morning German,
not far from Stenger's Cafe
where smiling tiny women with string bags
filled with onions and limes
drink their Hudepohls at ten o'clock in the morning,
not far, on the one hand, from mute agonies of poverty,
abuse, addiction, ill-health, abandonment, drugs,
and, on the other,
long healthy dwellings-in-place, rootedness,
kitchens fragrant with onions, sausages,
pot roast, basins of steaming chittlins,
good talk and history part of every day,
kin and memories up and down the blocks,
not far from the front stoop on which blaze two late pots
of red loud geraniums, or the upstairs windows
curtained in tea-stained lace, or the well-dressed
black man shopping for eggs.
Not far from all this, I walk and watch, I take it in.
City,
you are a cornucopia of contradictions—
the bright Jaguar turning the corner
past the Alabama Fish House
with steamed-up windows, its paint peeling
like the buntings of regret,
faded advertising mumbling
"Free Lunch On Your Birthday,"
the prostitute waiting
in her leopard coat and blood-scarlet lips,
the priest passing on his way to Mass,
truants blowing reefer
on the second floors of broken-backed buildings,
grandmothers sitting down to biscuits
and gravy and talkative husbands,
neighborhoods of fear with secret dogs

in every doorway, huddled kids singing hip-hop carols
on stoplight honking crowded dancing sidewalks:

I study you, city, hang in your alleys,
lurk in your cul de sacs, tramp
your long avenues, walk wary your flooded
and littered precincts: I slouch when you slouch,
I sprint from the cops when you sprint from the cops,
I sit down in the dark with you
in some tiny candle-lit brick courtyard at midnight;
like Walt Whitman when he steamed here on the river,
(leaving his voice for me and for this poem,
gift of omnivorous catalog and endless grass-spiced breath)
I pause with you as with a lover;
I sip your honeyed night-dark tea.

But now, this autumn brilliant smoky morning
I enter the storefront Saigon Market,
its abundant nooks fishy, spiced,
drifting herbal currents and eddies
of air from windowed coolers and cubbies.
The owner chopsticks noodles from a bowl
while he listens to Dolly Parton,
and I see that heaven and health and goodness
are gathered in jars in this place,
that here for us, jeweled in glass and arrayed,
are the fruits of our once-enemies,
Vietnamese, Cambodians, Chinese, Japanese,
enemies we strafed, burned, atomized,
displaced even as they did much the same to us,
forced marches, pungi sticks, booby traps
that reaped us of our arms and legs and eyes—
I see all the better harvests here now,
offered as if in exchange,
offered in peaceable commerce.

O history,
you too have your thousand menus,
serve up your courses of horror
and hatred, annihilations, mass graves,
firebombings, blitzkriegs, sieges, sabotage,

ethnic cleansings, coups d'etat,
bombings, assassinations,
bright kamikaze blossoms
decorating the decks of crowded ships,
hidden minings and torpedoings,
a billion explosive unwedgings of the joints of bodies,
a billion collapsings of bridges and skulls and families,
a billion orphanings, a billion fratricides and patricides,
a billion wordless forgotten soul-wrecking
agonies of imprisonments.

Now here, as if in attempted compensation,
(I choose to see it so, as Walt would choose to think
it well after bloodthirsty ages of mayhem)
as if to offer self-amnesties to all
of us who have sinned,
gifts for the wounded and not wounded,
I see presented before us
the harvests of Vietnamese paddy
and Korean forest
side by side with those riches of our places—
North Carolina woods,
eastern Kentucky hollows,
southern Ohio fields and New England marshes—
which feed us all now, brothers and sisters,
kin in the eating and drinking and preparing,
kin in the kitchen skills, chopping, cleaning,
braising, frying, boiling, shredding and reconstituting,
feeding together on the fruits of the world we share,
heal-alls of all sorts: ginseng, from Korea or China,
panax quinquefolia, Five-Leafed Heal-All,
the same ginseng my friend Roger Swartz's dad
collected in the woods outside Steubenville
then dried in his garage next to his pickup truck,
and then sold later for good money
to buy whatever else he needed for good health;
the same ginseng Chinese raiders, with the Viet Cong,
carried in their pockets along the Ho Chi Minh Trail
as they sallied southward in search of my brother to kill him.
But I see here too, on these American shelves, plain-hewn
of timber that great ships might be built of,

Goldenseal Root, Yohimbe Powder,
Bee Pollen and White Elder Flower,
here Sea Palmetto Berry, Blue Vervain, Black Cohosh,
here Marshmallow Root,
here Slippery Elm Bark, here Butcher's Broom,
Borage, Skullcap Herb,
here Dandelion Root, here Squaw Vine Root,
and I am lost for a moment in sweet odors,
choirs of names, nominations of beauty and health
incarnate in earthy powders, siftings and grindings
of verdigris, saffron, rouge, siena, burnt umber—
all the hues of growing things and remedies,
all heart medicines, tonics, relaxants, rubifascients,

food if not for the body then food for the spirit,
food for the mind to set before itself,
repast of word and memory,
forgiveness and healths all around,
new history and new goodness
beginning with every meal—
and Walt beside me, his amplifications like
the menu of some great feast of *omnes omnes omnes*,
I want to join the great table of the city,
set by all of us at meal together,
and invoke a simple blessing:

gather and eat be good to one another take care.

The Evening Toast   by David A. Petreman

From the silence of asparagus
Sea bass and puréed potatoes
Francisco takes me down
Another unfamiliar road
When he lifts his glass.

I reach for mine,
Measure the balance
Between the flow
Of white wine
And the spillage of words.

This time he begins with oxen
Lying in the folds
Of Chiloé hills, the only
Movement their mouths
Grinding wild grasses.

He brings up sheep
From the Patagonian pampa
And cattle from the deep south
Who always ruminate alone.

It is my own chewing
That bothers me, he says,
It reminds me too much
Of my own skeleton.

We stare at each other,
Sip and swirl wine
To cleanse our mouths.

Bowing our heads,
We resume eating softly,
Listen for the click-click
Of teeth and bones.

FAT POEM   **by David Citino**

Late in the Paleolithic, before

this sumptuous ease, because their first need was *Flee,*

beasts stayed lean. Life was thin, *Chase, make haste.* We ran

and hid for our few good tastes, the breast, a fresh kill steaming

the hard, inhospitable stars. Now, a billion hens laying their stoned days away,

fetid feedlots deep with DES and marbled prime, hogs too gross to breed

without helping human hands, neurotic calves penned to the dark, what

we ache for, *Crave, crave*, because of what we used to be

and what we are, is good enough

to break our hearts.

Neighbor   **by Herbert Woodward Martin**

Spring is in you
Gentle old Jew
You knew isolated hungers
Like no other communal stomach.
Gentle Sir, you gathered
Dispensable chicken parts,
Carefully cooked and seasoned them,
Then fed the tribe of cats at your back door.
Gentle man, your house is empty now.
The cats, themselves, are
Dispersed like the wind searching
For the unimaginable corners
Of your generous hands.

Leningrad   by Natasha Sajé

I've heard stories about hunger:
my mother begging for turnips for two years,
my father roasting the tongues
of his boots when the war ended.
But neither had it as bad as the people
in Leningrad, sieged for nine hundred days, three winters
without food. They traded diamond rings
and icons for meat patties. Human meat,
slightly sweet like horseflesh, though fattier.
I know it's easy to lose one's hunger:
after days, it deepens to a dull ache,
and after weeks of eating nothing,
the body's used itself
for fuel, and food's as foreign as plastic.
But when instead of fasting you eat a little,
you remain ravenous, conscious
of sour breath and the stomach as an open sore,
and eager to admit that everything feeds
on something in this world.
For that admission, nothing expiates, not
the weekly air lift, not
parks lined by avenues of birches, not
voices in candlelit chapels,
and not summers
bathed in long, milky, northern light.

Communion in the Asylum   by Andrew Hudgins

We kneel. Some of us kneel better than others
and do not have to clutch the rail or sway
against those next to us. We hold up hands
to take the body in, and some of our hands
—a few—are firmer than the others. They
don't tremble, don't have to be held in the priest's
encircling hands and guided to our lips.

And some of us can hold the wafer, all of it,
inside our mouths. And when the careful priest
tips wine across our lips, many of us, for reverence,
don't moan or lurch or sing songs to ourselves.
But we all await the grace that's promised us.

Black Cherry Ice Cream at Mercy Hospice   by Clarinda Harriss
for Bonnie, 1938-2002

Sweet sister in innocent sins
like parking in the woods to smoke
with varsity boys in letter sweaters,
the blackheart cherry print
of your lips on wicked cigarettes
would've shaken the unshockable
Quakers of Friends School 'Fifty-Six
more if they knew we flirted with love-
less touch, pure in its sensuality.
We were reading *Return of the Native*.
We liked that path where Eustacia Vye
doubled back so a low-hanging limb
could stroke her hair again.
Thomas Hardy girls, you and I.

The pink stains on the paper
napkin labeled "Mercy"
(Butt-ends of our days and ways)
mock those redhot lipstick prints.
I slide black cherry ice cream
between thin integumental lines
incapable now of forming words.
The purity of the senses
in this senseless-seeming feeding
dazzles my eyebones like a knife
of ice, white as light. You like it.
It won't stay your cancer death
a day, an hour, a morphine minute.
You lean to the spoon. Cool. Sweet.

"Poverty Sucks"   by Maggie Jaffe

"We have the right
not to know about the poor,"
my student wrote
after I showed the class
photos of people working,
specifically a Haitian cane-cutter,
propped up on his scythe, dead
asleep on his feet.
This particular cane-cutter
earns 5 *gourdes* for 10 hours,
approximately one dollar a day.
With luck he'll live to be 54:
in Haiti the sun is boss
as well as the bosses.
My student vacations in the Bahamas,
sips his *Cuba Libre,*
eyes the girls, tans, doesn't see
the sweating Blacks.
Has never seen anyone sweat
at work: not on TV, in videos, in movies.
I should give him no more than a " **D**"
—as in **d**ollars **d**isseminate **d**eath—
but he still wouldn't *get* it:
that a man can be so broke
he falls asleep on his feet.

Poppies   by Maggie Jaffe

> *lull all pain and anger, bring*
> *forgetfulness of every sorrow.*
> —Homer, *The Odyssey*

Crossing into California
from Arizona, the border guard
asks where I was born.

New York, I answer.
Say something in English, he says.
Something in English, I retort.
That's not what I say, staring
at his magnificent 9mm
Sig Sauer in its shiny leather holster.

Kali/fornia. Blood-orange
poppy, the state flower,
freshly built prisons and road
signs' warnings about hitchhikers.
"Easy does it," fat-free thighs,
mud slides, earthquake, rebellion,
fire—in California, you'll want
to live forever.

Interstate 8 razors the Mojave
with the precision of a Hollywood
Mogul's line of coke. Sky shot
through with bars of color,
girlie pink and baby blue.
Behind us and closing
fast, an avocado-
green immigration van.

A Poem for Will, Baking   by Susan Rich

Each night he stands before
the kitchen island, begins again
from scratch: chocolate, cinnamon, nutmeg,
he beats, he folds;
keeps faith in what happens
when you combine known quantities,
bake twelve minutes at a certain heat.
The other rabbis, the scholars,
teenagers idling by the beach,
they receive his offerings,

in the early hours, share his grief.
It's enough now, they say.
Each day more baked goods to friends,
and friends of friends, even
the neighborhood cops. He can't stop,
holds on to the rhythmic opening
and closing of the oven,
the timer's expectant ring.
I was just baking, he says if
someone comes by. Again and again,
evenings winter into spring,
he creates the most fragile
of confections: madelines
and pinwheels, pomegranate crisps
and blue florentines;
each crumb to reincarnate
a woman – a savoring
of what the living once could bring.

Milkfish   by Eugene Gloria

You feed us milkfish stew
and long grain rice, make us eat
blood soup with chili peppers,
and frown at us when we lose our appetite.
I remember when I was young and you told me
of that monsoon: the Japanese Occupation—
stories of a time before you met my father,
when you learned the language of an occupied city
in order to feed your family.
You were the pretty one at seventeen,
your skin, white as milkfish.
The pretty ones, you said,
were always given more food—
the Japanese soldiers sentried
above the loft where you worked
dropped sweet yams, and you caught them
by the billow of your skirt.

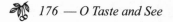

I remember you in sepia-brown photographs
as a mestiza who equated liberation
with Hershey bars and beige nylons from American Gis—
and the season of the monsoon as dark as hunger
was not about suffering
but what you knew of beauty.

The Cookie Poem   by Jeff Gundy

"Here are my sad cookies."

The sad cookies. The once and future cookies.
The broken sweet cookies. The cookies
of heartbreaking beauty. The stony cookies
of Palestine. The gummy and delicious
olive and honey cookie. The pasty
damp cookie trapped in the child's hand.

Sad cookies, weird cookies, slippery
and dangerous cookies. Brilliant helpless
soiled and torn cookies, feverish and sweaty
cookies. Sullen cookies, sassy cookies,
the cookies of tantrum and the cookie of joy
and the sweet dark cookie of peace.

The faithful cookie of Rotterdam. The wild-eyed
cookie of Münster. The salty Atlantic cookie.
Cookies in black coats, in coveralls,
in business suits, cookies in bonnets
and coverings and heels, cookies scratching
their heads and their bellies, cookies utterly
and shamelessly naked before the beloved.

Cookies of the Amish division, cookies
of the Wahlerhof, cookies of Zurich and
Strassburg and Volhynia and Chortitza,
Nairobi Djakarta Winnipeg Goshen.
Cookies who hand their children off
to strangers, who admonish their sons

to remember the Lord's Prayer, cookies
who say all right, baptize my children
and then sneak back to the hidden church anyway.
Cookies who cave in utterly. Cookies
who die with their boots on. Cookies
with fists, and with contusions.
The black hearted cookie. The cookie with issues.
Hard cookies, hot cookies, compassionate
conservative cookies, cookies we loathe
and love, cookies lost, fallen, stolen,
crushed, abandoned, shunned. Weary
and heroic cookies, scathingly noted cookies,
flawed cookies who did their best.
Single cookies, queer cookies, cookies of color,
homeless cookie families sleeping in the car,
obsolete cookies broken down on the information
highway. Sad cookies, silent cookies,
loud cookies, loved cookies, your cookies
my cookies our cookies, all cookies
God's cookies, strange sweet hapless cookies
marked each one by the Imago Dei,
oh the Father the Son the Mother the Daughter
and the Holy Ghost all love cookies,
love all cookies, God's mouth is full
of cookies, God chews and swallows and flings
hands wide in joy, the crumbs fly
everywhere, oh God loves us all.

After the Reunion   **by David Baker**

To finish by picking up pieces of cake and small clutter
from the sunporch floor, to finish by cleaning up.

We couldn't tell them—not the host of relatives
happy to be on each other's hands again,

                               each other's nerves.
The lilac hedge let go its whole bushel of odors

and our acre's birds kept stitching the trees
with their art. Everyone said so.

Someone's boss is somebody's neighbor.
Who looks like who in the crisp old albums?

—What kind of linen, what brand of seed, what
do you do when things get bad?

                    There is nothing
that does not connect and so sustain.

And now I want us to keep trying to love each other, too.
The strength it takes is their patience—

a stretching of legs, waiting long.
Who knows what sadnesses they have endured?

Who knows which ones we have caused?
Let's open the door and let the bluejays and sparrows

weep while we clean. Let's take the whole day.
Let's keep forever the napkin our last waving aunt

pressed her kiss into—delicate red, already
powdered, doomed as a rose . . .

Sustenance   **by Ralph Black**

For an hour there is nothing
but rain on the stones, trillings of light
that signal a world into being.

For an hour there is only this hunger—
twilight settling into the trees, a bird
whose song I do not know, vanishing.

In an hour I will be home,
my jacket thrown onto the couch,
my wet shoes kicked off at the door.

Later, sipping wine in the kitchen,
watching candelight refract in the
burn-sienna prisms of Chilean cabernet,

I will lift the large knife and lean
into the apple, fruit of New Zealand,
fruit of Madagascar, halving, quartering,

eighth- and sixteenth-ing it open—
this good, widely divisible world.
The walnuts from Jerusalem, green onions

from Spain, and then, if ripe, that visceral avocado.
I will sing to my daughter while stirring
the balsamic into the first cold-pressed
pressing of oil, grinding the pepper
as my voice grinds out the song,
doing the artichoke dance that she loves.

And when I say to my daughter say grace
she says *grace*, gracefully, gratefully,
a word for it sung into the air.

That we eat of what is given, these few
resilient gifts of a day, that we bow and eat
and watch the world for signs of who we are:

vanishing bird, circles and circles,
the rain perhaps slowing, perhaps
gaining on us all over again.

At Twig's End
by Cathryn Essinger

In the back bedroom, my son is writing a novel.
He has already *cleared the sill of the world*,
and is no longer *battling against the brilliance*.

I can feel the words forming around him,
the way rainwater moves the length of a branch
before collecting into a droplet at twig's end.

He hangs suspended between worlds, testing
shaky terrain, making little leaps into the unknown,
then backtracking to see how far he has come.

In the rhythm of the keys, I can hear the rumble
of city streets, the click of a subway, a door finding
its own latch, the tap of a cigarette in a lonely room.

When I call him to dinner, he rises and comes
to the table, but I can see from the look in his eyes
that he can't quite remember who we are

and why have we called him away? I want to remind
him that I, too, have been lost in this world
where we linger, half-afraid of who we might become,

but I fill him a plate instead and send him back
to his work, where I know I will find him later, tipped
back in his chair, one hand balancing his supper,

the other fingering the keys, still searching
for the right words, while the meal I prepared,
meat and potatoes, grows cold on the plate.

(Italics indicate borrowed lines from Richard Wilbur's "The Writer.")

The Cleaving   by Li-Young Lee

He gossips like my grandmother, this man
with my face, and I could stand
amused all afternoon
in the Hon Kee Grocery,
amid hanging meats he
chops: roast pork cut
from a hog hung
by nose and shoulders,
her entire skin burnt
crisp, flesh I know
to be sweet,
her shining
face grinning
up at ducks
dangling single file,
each pierced by black hooks through breast, bill,
and steaming from a hole
stitched shut at the ass.
I step to the counter, recite,
and he, without even slightly
varying the rhythm of his current confession or harangue,
scribbles my order on a greasy receipt,
and chops it up quick.

Such a sorrowful Chinese face,
nomad, Gobi, Northern
in its boniness
clear from the high
warlike forehead
to the sheer edge of the jaw.
He could be my brother, but finer,
and, except for his left forearm, which is engorged,
sinewy from his daily grip and
wield of a two-pound tool,
he's delicate, narrow-
waisted, his frame
so slight a lover, some
rough other

might break it down
its smooth, oily length.
In his light-handed calligraphy
on receipts and in his
moodiness, he is
a Southerner from a river-province;
suited for scholarship, his face poised
above an open book, he'd mumble
his favorite passages.
He could be my grandfather;
come to America to get a Western education
in 1917, but too homesick to study,
he sits in the park all day, reading poems
and writing letters to his mother.

He lops the head off, chops
the neck of the duck
into six, slits
the body
open, groin
to breast, and drains
the scalding juices,
then quarters the carcass
with two fast hacks of the cleaver,
old blade that has worn
into the surface of the round
foot-thick chop-block
a scoop that cradles precisely the curved steel.

The head, flung from the body, opens
down the middle where the butcher
cleanly halved it between
the eyes, and I
see fetal-crouched
inside the skull, the homunculus,
gray brain grainy
to eat.
Did this animal, after all, at the moment
its neck broke,
image the way his executioner
shrinks from his own death?

Is this how
I, too, recoil from my day?
See how this shape
hordes itself, see how
little it is.
See its grease on the blade.
Is this how I'll be found
when judgment is passed, when names
are called, when crimes are tallied?
This is also how I looked before I tore my mother open.
Is this how I presided over my century, is this how
I regarded the murders?
This is also how I prayed.
Was it me in the Other
I prayed to when I prayed?
This too was how I slept, clutching my wife.
Was it me in the other I loved
when I loved another?
The butcher sees me eye this delicacy.
With a finger, he picks it
out of the skull-cradle
and offers it to me.
I take it gingerly between my fingers
and suck it down.
I eat my man.

The noise the body makes
when the body meets
the soul over the soul's ocean and penumbra
is the old sound of up-and-down, in-and-out,
a lump of muscle chug-chugging blood
into the ear; a lover's
heart-shaped tongue;
flesh rocking flesh until flesh comes;
the butcher working
at his block and blade to marry their shapes
by violence and time;
an engine crossing,
re-crossing salt water, hauling
immigrants and the junk
of the poor. These are the faces I love, the bodies

and scents of bodies
for which I long
in various ways, at various times,
thirteen gathered around the redwood,
happy talkative, voracious
at day's end,
eager to eat
four kinds of meat
prepared four different ways,
numerous plates and bowls of rice and vegetables,
each made by distinct affections
and brought to table by many hands.

Brothers and sisters by blood and design,
who sit in separate bodies of varied shapes,
we constitute a many-membered
body of love.
In a world of shapes
of my desires, each one here
is a shape of one of my desires, and each
is known to me and clear by virtue
of each one's unique corruption
of those texts, the face, the body:
that jut jaw
to gnash tendon;
that wide nose to meet the blows
a face like that invites;
those long eyes closing on the seen;
those thick lips
to suck the meat of animals
or recite 300 poems of the T'ang;
these teeth to bite my monosyllables;
these cheekbones to make
those syllables sing the soul.
Puffed or sunken
according to the life,
dark or light according
to the birth, straight
or humped, whole, manqué, quasi, each pleases, verging
on utter grotesquery.
All are beautiful by variety.

The soul too
is a debasement
of a text, but, thus, it
acquires salience, although a
human salience, but
inimitable, and, hence, memorable.
God is the text.
The soul is a corruption
and a mnemonic.

A bright moment,
I hold up an old head
from the sea and admire the haughty
down-curved mouth
that seems to disdain
all the eyes are blind to,
including me, the eater.
Whole unto itself, complete
without me, yet its
shape complements the shape of my mind.
I take it as text and evidence
of the world's love for me,
and I feel urged to utterance,
urged to read the body of the world, urged
to say it
in human terms,
my reading a kind of eating, my eating
a kind of reading,
my saying a diminishment, my noise
a love-in-answer.
What is it in me would
devour the world to utter it?
What is it in me will not let
the world be, would eat
not just this fish,
but the one who killed it,
the butcher who cleaned it.
I would eat the way he
squats, the way he
reaches into the plastic tubs
and pulls out a fish, clubs it, takes it

to the sink, guts it, drops it on the weighing pan.
I would eat that thrash
and plunge of the watery body
in the water, that liquid violence
between the man's hands.
I would eat
the gutless twitching on the scales,
three pounds of dumb nerve and pulse, I would eat it all
to utter it.
The deaths at the sinks, those bodies prepared
for eating, I would eat,
and the standing deaths
at the counters, in the aisles,
the walking deaths in the streets,
the death-far-from-home, the death-
in-a-strange-land, these Chinatown
deaths, these American deaths.
I would devour this race to sing it,
this race that according to Emerson
managed to preserve to a hair
for three or four thousand years
the ugliest features in the world.
I would eat these features, eat
the last three or four thousand years, every hair.
And I would eat Emerson, his transparent soul, his
soporific transcendence.
I would eat this head,
glazed in pepper-speckled sauce,
the cooked eyes opaque in their sockets.
I bring it to my mouth and—
the way I was taught, the way I've watched
others before me do—
with a stiff tongue lick out
the cheek-meat and the meat
over the armored jaw, my eating,
its sensual, salient nowness,
punctuating the void
from which such hunger springs and to which it proceeds.

And what
is this

I excavate
with my mouth?
What is this
plated, ribbed, hinged
architecture, this *carp head*,
but one more
articulation of a single nothing
severally manifested?
What is my eating,
rapt as it is,
but another shape of going,
my immaculate expiration?

O, nothing is so
steadfast it won't go
the way the body goes.
The body goes.
The body's grave,
so serious
in its dying,
arduous as martyrs
in that task and as
glorious. It goes
empty always
and announces its going
by spasms and groans, farts and sweats.

What I thought were the arms
aching *cleave*, were the knees trembling *leave*.
What I thought were the muscles
insisting *resist, persist, exist,*
were the pores
hissing *mist* and *waste*.
What I thought was the body humming *reside, reside,*
was the body sighing *revise, revise.*
O, the murderous deletions, the keening
down to nothing, the cleaving.
All of the body's revisions end
in death.
All of the body's revisions end.

Bodies eating bodies, heads eating heads,
we are nothing eating nothing,
and though we feast,
are filled, overfilled,
we go famished.
We gang the doors of death.
That is, our deaths are fed
that we may continue our daily dying,
our bodies going
down, while the plates-soon-empty
are passed around, that true
direction of our true prayers,
while the butcher spells
his message, manifold,
in the mortal air.
He coaxes, cleaves, brings change
before our very eyes, and at every
moment of our being.
As we eat we're eaten.
Else what is this violence, this salt, this
passion, this heaven?

I thought the soul an airy thing.
I did not know the soul
is cleaved so that the soul might be restored.
Live wood hewn,
its sap springs from a sticky wound.
No seed, no egg has he
whose business calls for an axe.
In the trade of my soul's shaping,
he traffics in hews and hacks.

No easy thing, violence.
One of its names? Change. Change
resides in the embrace
of the effaced and the effacer,
in the covenant of the opened and the opener;
the axe accomplishes it on the soul's axis.
What then may I do
but cleave to what cleaves me.
I kiss the blade and eat my meat.

I thank the wielder and receive,
while terror spirits
my change, sorrow also.

The terror the butcher
scripts in the unhealed
air, the sorrow of his Shang
dynasty face,
African face with slit eyes. He is my sister, this
beautiful Bedouin, this Shulamite,
keeper of sabbaths, diviner
of holy texts, this dark
dancer, this Jew, this Asian, this one
with the Cambodian face, Vietnamese face, this Chinese
I daily face,
this immigrant,
this man with my own face.

CREDITS & ACKNOWLEDGMENTS

Maggie Anderson, "Recurring" from her *Cold Comfort*, © 1986, and "Soup" from her *A Space Filled with Moving*, © 1992. Permission of Univ. of Pittsburgh Press.

Jimmy Santiago Baca, "Green Chile" from *Black Mesa Poems*, copyright © 1989 by Jimmy Santiago Baca. Reprinted by permission of New Directions Publishing Corp.

David Baker, "After the Reunion," from his *After the Reunion* (U of Arkansas Press, 1994).

Gail Bellamy, "Lunch Dates" from *Food Poems* (Bottom Dog Press, 2000).

Wendell Berry, "Winter Nightfall" & "February 2, 1968" from *Collected Poems: 1957-1982* by Wendell Berry. Copyright © Reprinted by permission of North Point Press, a division of Farrar, Straus & Giroux. LLC.

Elizabeth Bishop, "Sestina" from *The Complete Poems*, 1927-1979 by Elizabeth Bishop. Copyright © 1979, 1983 by Alice Helen Methfessel. Reprinted by permission of Farrar, Straus & Giroux, LLC.

Louise Bogan, "To Wine" from *The Blue Estuaries, Poems 1923-1968.* Permission of Ecco Press.

Don Bogen, "Learning to Clam," from his *After the Splendid Display* (Wesleyan UP, 1986).

Imogene Bolls, "The Little Permanence" from *Earthbound: Ohio Women Poems* (Bottom Dog Press, 1989).

Grace Butcher, "My Mother and the Bums" from *Child, House, World*, © Grace Butcher, Hiram Poetry Review Series, 1991.

Jared Carter, "What I Thought I Was Eating." Copyright © 1984 by Jared Carter. First published in *Pembroke Review*.

Daryl Ngee Chinn, "Words, Like Rice and Snow" from his *Soft Parts of the Back* (Gainesville: UP of Florida).

David Citino, "Fat Poem," from his *Broken Symmetry* (Columbus: Ohio State UP, 1997).

Billy Collins, "Litany," from his *Nine Horses*, copyright © 2002 by Billy Collins. Used by permission of Random House, Inc.

Edmund Conti, "Summer Haiku" and "Blueberries" were first published in the New Jersey Section of the *New York Sunday Times*.

Paola Corso, "End Pieces," from her *A Proper Burial* (Johnstown, OH: Pudding House, 2003).

Barbara Crooker, "My Mother's Pie Crust," first published in *Literary Lunch (Kentucky Writers Group)*.

James Cummins, "Reading Hemingway," first published in *Kenyon Review*.

Mark Doty, "A Display of Mackerel" from *Atlantis.* © 1995. Permission of Harper Collins.

Rita Dove, "Sunday Greens," from her *Thomas and Beulah* (Carnegie-Mellon UP), © 1986 by Rita Dove.

Erica Jong, "The Woman Who Loved to Cook," copyright © 1973, 2001, Erica
Mann Jong, used by permission of the poet.

Susan Kelly-DeWitt, "Salt," from her *To a Small Moth* (Poet's Corner Press, 2001).

Terry Kirts, "Macaroni & Cheese Survey," first published in *Gastronomica* 3.1
(2003): 14-15.

Karen Kovacik, "The Art of Love," first published in *The Cape Rock*.

Li-Young Lee, "The Weight of Sweetness" from his *Rose* (BOA Editions, Ltd.,
1986). "The Cleaving," from his *The City in Which I Love You* (BOA
Editions, Ltd. 1990).

Denise Levertov, "O Taste and See" from *Poems 1960-67*, copyright © 1964 by
Denise Levertov. Reprinted by permission of New Directions Publishing
Corp.

Julia Levine, "Hunting Wild Mushrooms" from her *Practicing for Heaven*.
Copyright © 1999, Anhinga Press.

Stuart Lishan, "Song of Separation 2," first published in *Kenyon Review* 20.1
(Winter, 1998): 103-104; "The Cake," first published in *Barrow Street*
(Summer, 2000).

John Logan, "Avocado" from *John Logan: The Collected Poems*. Copyright ©
1989 by the John Logan Literary Estate. Reprinted with the permission of
BOA Editions, Ltd.

Daniel Lusk, "Understudy," first published in *Dakotah Territory*.

Rebecca McClanahan, "Produce Aisle" from her *Mrs. Houdini* (UP of Florida).

Colleen J. McElroy, "To Market, To Market" from her *Bone Flames* (Wesleyan UP,
1984).

Christopher Merrill, from "Pike Place Market Variations" in his *Watch Fire* (White
Pine Press, 1994).

W.S. Merwin, excerpts from "Korean Figures," "Philippine Figures," and "Chinese
Figures I" from *East Window: The Asian Translations*. Copyright © 1998
by W. S. Merwin. Reprinted with the permission of Copper Canyon Press,
P. O. Box 271, Port Townsend, WA 98368-0271.

W.S. Merwin, "The Clover," from his *The Miner's Pale Children*. Copyright © 1970
W.S. Merwin, reprinted with permission of The Wylie Agency, Inc.

Frank O'Hara, "A Step Away from Them" from his *Lunch Poems* (San Francisco:
City Lights Books, 1995).

David Petreman, "The Evening Toast," first published in *Tampa Review* 8 (1994).

Deanna Pickard, "The Story of Butter," first published in *Chelsea*.

Susan Azar Porterfield, "Kibbe," first published in *North American Review*.

Lynn Powell, "At Ninety-Eight," from *Old and New Testament* © Lynn Powell.
Permission from U of Wisconsin.

Kevin Prufer, "Adolescence," reprinted from *The Finger Bone* by permission of
Carnegie Mellon University Press © 2002 by Kevin Prufer.

Susan Rich, "A Poem for Will, Baking," first published in *Prism International*.

Karen Rigby, "Borscht," first published in the December 14, 2002 edition of *The
Pittsburgh Post-Gazette*.

Pattiann Rogers, "Murder in the Good Land" from her *Song of the World Becom-
ing: New and Collected Poems, 1981-2001* (Minneapolis: Milkweed

Editions, 2001). Copyright © 2001 by Pattiann Rogers. Reprinted by permission of Milkweed Editions.

Ira Sadoff, "My Last Two Wives" from *Settling Down* (Houghton Mifflin, 1975). Used by permission of the author.

Natasha Sajé, "Leningrad" from his *Red Under the Skin* © 1994 by Natasha Sajé. Reprinted by permission of the University of Pittsburgh Press.

Vivian Shipley, "Ode on a Beet," from her *Crazy Quilt* (Newtown, Ct: Hanover Press, 1999).

Martha Silano, "Sweet Red Peppers, Sun-Drieds, the Hearts of Artichokes," from her *What the Truth Tastes Like* (Nightshade Press, 1999).

Charles Simic, "The Spoon" & "Fork" & "Watermelons" from his *Dismantling the Silence*. Copyright © Charles Simic. Used by permission of George Brazillier Publishing.

Kay Sloan, "Breakfast at Keseberg's Diner," first published in *The Paris Review* (summer, 1994).

Francis Smith, "Table for One," first published in *Light Year* (Cleveland: Bits Press, 1986).

Larry Smith, "The Baking" from his *Scissors, Paper, Rock* (Cleveland State University Poetry Center, 1982).

Ann Stanford, "The Blackberry Thicket" from *The Weathercock*. Used by permission of Penguin Books.

Gertrude Stein, "Food," from *Tender Buttons* (L. A.: Sun & Moon Press, 1991).

Gerald Stern, "Grapefruit" from *Finding Another Kingdom: Selected Poems*. Copyright © 1990. Used by permission of the poet.

Joyce Sutphen, "Ever After," first published in *Poetry* (February, 2003).

F. Richard Thomas, "Two Lives: Making Supper at Lake George" from his *Death at Camp Pahoka* (Michigan State UP, 2000).

Ann Townsend, "Nectar," from her *Dime Store Erotics* (Silverfish Review Press, 1998).

Pamela Uschuk, "Finding Peaches in the Desert" from her *Finding Peaches in the Desert*, Wings Press, San Antonio, TX, © 2000.

Diane Wakoski, "Ode to a Lebanese Crock of Olives" from her *Emerald Ice: Selected Poems, 1962-1987* (Black Sparrow Press).

Michael Waters, "Black Olives," first published in *Poetry* (June, 2002).

Gabriel Welsch, "Preserves," first published in *Lucid Stone* (Spring, 2001).

Ingrid Wendt, "Mussels" from her *Singing in the Mozart Requiem* (Breitenbush Books, 1987), first published in *California* Quarterly (Spring/Summer, 1984); "Tiramasù" first published in *Old Oregon* 71.1 (Autumn, 1991).

William Carlos Williams, "This Is Just To Say" from his *Collected Poems: 1909-1939, Volume I*, copyright © 1938 by New Directions Publishing Corp. Reprinted by permission of New Directions Publishing Corp.

Steve Wilson, "The Beekeeper," first published in *The Christian Science Monitor*. Copyright © 2002 by Steve Wilson.

James Wright, "Northern Pike," from *Above the River: The Complete Poems* (1990), by permission of Wesleyan University Press.

The Editors

David Lee Garrison was born in Bremerton, Washington, and educated at Wesleyan and Johns Hopkins Universities. After visiting appointments at Indiana University and the University of Kansas, he began teaching Spanish and Portuguese in 1979 at Wright State University (Dayton, Ohio), where he now chairs the Department of Modern Languages. He has taught creative writing workshops at Wright State and also at Antioch University, Sinclair Community College, and the University of Dayton. His work—poetry, criticism, fiction, reviews, and translations—has appeared in journals such as *Colorado Review, Kansas Quarterly, The Literary Review, Poem,* and *The Nation*, as well as in various anthologies. He has published two chapbooks, *Blue Oboe* (Wyndham Hall Press) and *Inside the Sound of Rain* (Vincent Brothers), and three volumes of translation, most recently *Certain Chance*, by Spanish poet Pedro Salinas (Bucknell University Press, 2000). Learning to cook for himself as a young single man led to his special interest in food and food poems. He lives in Dayton, Ohio, with his wife, Suzanne Kelly-Garrison, an attorney and fiction writer.

Terry Hermsen lives, gardens and cooks in Delaware, Ohio, with his wife Leslie and their two adopted children, Noel and Noah. For 25 years he has conducted poetry residencies in schools across Ohio, taking students into factories and prairies, zoos and museums. He has two chapbooks from Bottom Dog Press, *Child Aloft in Ohio Theatre* and *36 Spokes: The Bicycle Poems*. In 2003 he finished his dissertation in Art Education, looking at how poetry and art can help students more passionately connect with the world around them.

He would also dedicate this book, "To my oldest daughter, Isa, whom I taught how to cook—and who taught me back all the spices..."

Cover of *Food Poems: Pocket Poems #1*
Bottom Dog Press
Cover art by Allen Frost

****** Working Lives Series ******
Bottom Dog Press
http://members.aol.com/lsmithdog/bottomdog

Robert Flanagan. *Loving Power: Stories.* 1990
0-933087-17-9 $8.95
A Red Shadow of Steel MIlls: Photos and Poems. 1991
(Includes Timothy Russell, David Adams, Kip Knott, Richard Hague)
0-933087-18-7 $8.95
Chris Llewellyn. *Steam Dummy & Fragments from the Fire: Poems.* 1993
0-933087-29-2 $8.95
Larry Smith. *Beyond Rust: Stories.* 1996 / 0-933087-39-X $9.95
Getting By: Stories of Working Lives. 1996
eds. David Shevin and Larry Smith / 0-933087-41-1 $10.95
Human Landscapes: Three Books of Poems. 1997
(Includes Daniel Smith, Edwina Pendarvis, Philip St. Clair)
0-933087-42-X $10.95
Richard Hague. *Milltown Natural: Essays and Stories from a Life.* 1997
0-933087-44-6 $16.95 (cloth)
Maj Ragain. *Burley One Dark Sucker Fired.* 1998
0-933087-45-4 $9.95
Brooding the Heartlands: Poets of the Midwest, ed. M.L.Liebler. 1998
0-933087-50-0 $9.95
Writing Work: Writers on Working-Class Writing. 1999
eds. David Shevin, Larry Smith, Janet Zandy / 0-933087-52-7 $10.95
Jim Ray Daniels. *No Pets: Stories.* 1999/ 0-933087-54-3 $10.95
Jeanne Bryner. *Blind Horse: Poems.* 1999 / 0-933087-57-8 $9.95
Naton Leslie. *Moving to Find Work: Poems.* 2000 / 0-933087-61-6 $9.95
David Kherdian. *The Neighborhood Years.* 2000 / 0-933087-62-4 $9.95
Our Working Lives: Short Stories of People and Work. 2000
eds. Bonnie Jo Campbell and Larry Smith / 0-933087-63-2 $12.95
Allen Frost. *Ohio Trio: Fictions.* 2001/ 0-933087-68-3 $10.95
Maj Ragain. *Twist the Axe: A Horseplayer's Story* 2002
0-933087-71-X $10.95
Michael Salinger. *Neon: Stories & Poems.* 2002 / 0-933087-72.1 $10.95
David Shevin. *Three Miles from Luckey: Poems.* 2002
0-933087-74-8 $10.95
*Working Hard for the Money: America's Working Poor in Stories, Poems, and
Photos.* 2002, eds. Mary E. Weems and Larry Smith
0-933087-77-2 $12.95
Eclipse: Stories by Jeanne Bryner. 2003 / 0-933087-78-0 $12.95